The Night and Nothing

The Night
and Nothing

BY GALE D. WEBBE

 NEW YORK · 1964

To the Glory of God

and in memory of Florence Menter

Acknowledgments

The late Dean Harton has left many of us Anglicans in a dilemma. We must either remain silent on the subject of Ascetics, or speak and write in commentary on his basic book *The Elements of the Spiritual Life.* Hence the only adequate way to express my obligation to Fr. Harton is to say that without reliance upon him this book could not have been written at all.

My chapter on Acedia acknowledges, in the text, its indebtedness to Bishop Paget's classic study. In addition the section owes much to the treatment of that subject in Bishop Mortimer's *The Elements of Moral Theology,* a sound Anglican manual in a rather neglected field.

To have known the Reverend Neil Stanley personally is one of my great privileges. However, in addition to his flashing intellect and sound scholarship he was a felicitous phrasemaker. His way of putting things still comes forth from my lips, and so it is certain that his shadow falls across these pages. Others who knew him will be glad that it does.

A whole generation of his students at the General Theological Seminary will recognize the influence of the Reverend Dr. Burton Scott Easton. Faulty memory makes impossible the extending of further individual credit to others whose thoughts, and possibly whose words, find expression here. I should be pleased to have these sources identified.

G. D. W.

Contents

Now when he had left speaking, he said unto Simon, Launch out into the deep, and let down your nets for a draught.

And Simon, answering, said unto him, Master, we have toiled all the night, and have taken nothing: nevertheless, at thy word I will let down the net.

Luke 5:4,5

Introduction

First love with God, like first love with a human being, usually involves such a tingling experience that we then feel fully alive for the first time. In sober truth we are. When, at our conversion, we abandon "the love of self for self," to use St Bernard of Clairvaux's classic phrase, we literally turn "from death unto life." It is characteristic—indeed it is proper—that for a while thereafter we enjoy some of the delights of this resurrection. In his happiness, as it were, that we have begun the essential process of loving beyond ourselves, God often rewards, and spurs, the venture by giving us many tangible gifts along with himself. Once more he says: "Bring forth the best robe, and put it on him; and put a ring on his hand, and shoes on his feet; and bring hither the fatted calf, and kill it; and let us eat, and be merry; for this my son was dead, and is alive again; he was lost, and is found" (Luke 15:22-3).

Like the original prodigal at his father's banquet, the newly converted are, often, thrillingly conscious of God in their eucharistic worship and Holy Communion. Their private prayer is, typically, a simple joy. Their entire rule of life is maintained without real difficulty. In general, the beginner on the spiritual journey walks side by side with God, almost taking it for granted that the road should smooth under his feet, that his questions should be answered while they are being voiced, that his problems should find solution before the evening comes.

While it is impossible to universalize in this matter, for there are indeed "varieties of religious experience," nevertheless it is also characteristic that this beginning phase of the spiritual life does not continue long. To limit illustrations to the devotional sphere, after a time the rule of life begins to be sheer hard work, unrewarded. Meditations become barren, yielding no fruit. In every fifteen minutes of prayer, as the mature St Teresa herself acknowledges, there are fourteen minutes of distraction. A general aridity settles over the soul, providing an excellent climate for the germination of seeds of doubt concerning the reality of religion. We begin to wonder if the spiritual life is merely an illusion. Mocking voices begin to whisper: "Peradventure God sleepeth, and must be awakened" (cf. 1 Kings 18:27). Shortly they are asserting, loudly and definitely, that God is dead.

To be equally dogmatic for the moment, this common experience in no way indicates that we have lost God, or he us. Religion has not failed. The living God, who neither slumbers nor sleeps, is still continuing his loving labors with the soul. If he seems to change his methods, it is only because our addiction to half-way houses forces him to deal with us by means of stern measures. His unaltering purpose is to bring all of us, at last, to that mysterious fullness of our being which St Bernard describes as "the love of self for God." Knowing that this potential development would be blighted if we were allowed merely to luxuriate forever in his gifts, he leads us to himself—and to ourself—through a featureless desert.

Again in St Bernard's terms, to reach the ultimate goal we must first move from the level of the "love of God for the sake of his gifts" to that of "love of God for himself." This book, as its title tries to indicate, is addressed to those who are engaged in this passage—they have reached the point where many, fearing the darkness, turn back to "company no more with him." Our intended readers, however, are persevering in their personal Exodus. Like their prototypes, the Israelites, they are penetrating ever more deeply into the inevitable wilderness that lies between the House of Bondage and the Promised Land. In their passage through this "barren and dry land where no water is" (Ps. 63:2), save the water of bitterness, they are encountering spiritual desolations of the most searching kind. They welcome every drop of moisture, however tepid, every gleam of light, however fitful, as they grope along.

Let it be said at once that their experience of dryness, rejection, darkness, and death is so universal in the normal course of spiritual development that it has technical names like "the Dark Night of the Soul." In addition, it is a recurring phenomenon. A person should fully expect to enter the shadows repeatedly, emerging each time on a higher level, as God continues to lead him on the spiritual journey. Indeed, great souls can become so familiar with "The Night and Nothing" that in it, far from becoming doubtful, resigned, or bitter, they look up and lift up their heads, knowing that when these things begin to come to pass their redemption draweth nigh (cf. Luke 21:28). They tell us that, precisely while we are in the very depths of our desolations, we should give thanks that God is honoring us by taking our initial resolve quite seriously, and is stopping at nothing in the process of making truly human beings of us. St. Paul is

spokesman for all of them when he writes: "I will glory of
the things which concern mine infirmities" (2 Cor. 11:30).

It is not merely being said herein that the spiritual life, too,
knows its darkness before dawn. While this is true in a measure, it is more important to note that God can be served just
as well in the darkness as in the day. Indeed, in a life
basically—and increasingly—lived by faith rather than by
sight the greater service is necessarily done by night.

Beyond that, however, the point is that the advancing soul
must ever be learning to say with Job, "Though he slay me,
yet will I trust in him" (Job 13:15). This note receives especial stress because of the universal human tendency to draw
false conclusions from the experience of spiritual desolations.
"I have always tried to live a good life; why does God do this
to me?" We must see our travails not as punishments but as
birthpangs attending the emergence of a "new creature"
who is evolving to the limit spiritually as well as merely
biologically. On no account should we abandon, or even level
off, the growth process that was begun when we made our
first fateful choice to place ourself into the hands of God to
be shaped into an instrument that could be of use in his purpose. We must continue, as willingly as is possible, to hold
the blade of the self against the whetstone of God, so that the
fine-edged tool he has in view may ultimately be produced.

The world has always stood in sore need of people who,
as a sure result of this painful perseverance, are filled "with
the Holy Ghost and with power" (Acts 10:38). Typically it
has not treated them well in their own generation, but
equally it has built monuments to them later on, thus
acknowledging a basic paradox of this sacramental world—
the fact that the otherworldly are precisely the ones who are
most really important in this present world.

The need for this sort of person has never been greater

than it is in our own day, when we have reached up and taken into our hands part of God. Now that we hold his power in our rather frightened grasp it is of the essence that we become possessed of other attributes of God, such as his wisdom and his love.

I Mortification

The process of "daily dying" connoted by the technical word "mortification," endured as it must be without benefit of sedation, provides sufficient agony even to the most thoroughly disciplined. A ready illustration is provided by the true story of an African missionary, who among his other trials was afflicted with the permanently crippling results of severe polio. One Sunday, while he was absent on his Father's business, his thatched hovel was burned to the ground. When he was carried back to the smoking ruins, which had contained every item of his scanty possessions save the clothes on his back, he was heard to observe, "God is teaching me detachment."

Quite possibly he experienced additional reactions. Certainly he illustrates the fact that "As dying, and behold we live" (2 Cor. 6:9) is not just a form of fine words. It states what is as searching a truth, when lived moment by moment, as we shall ever encounter. Its best pictorial representation is always the crucifix, which holds before our eyes a slow death on a lonely cross in the gathering darkness.

There are individuals who actually share, without a trace

of a martyr complex, a genuine vocation to this literal imita-
tion of Christ. Everybody has at least read about them, while
some of us have had the privilege of knowing one or two.
The overwhelming majority of us, however, are not called to
this dread privilege. The best we can aspire to is the grace to
undergo mortification fairly quietly because of our conviction
that no human soul can ever be really alive to God without
first being dead to this world.

"Conviction"? The word is far too strong. "Hypothesis"
is better. The spiritual beginner is aware that his Lord has
said (to everybody, not merely to a chosen few with the particular vocation to be Trappist monks), "Whosoever he be
of you that forsaketh not all that he hath, he cannot be my
disciple" (Luke 14:33). The willing spirit rejoices in Christ's
ennobling assumption that some humans at least, really wanting to become their perfect selves, will aspire to this absolute
heroism. His flesh, however, is weak. At the approach of the
personal fire it recoils from the slightest beginnings of mortification in actual practice, let alone that full measure of the
demanded forsaking which is to forsake without measure,
Thus is revealed, beyond any doubt, the uncomfortable truth
that his mind does not yet really assent to the fundamental
Christian proposition that we must "die in order to live."
How could it, when its patterns of thought have been
conditioned by centuries of contrary opinion? "Neither are
your ways my ways" indeed, and the western world, of which
our neophyte is the heir, has other teachings on how he may
best fulfill himself.
Each of us legitimately uses his life trying to be himself
and to be at home in the universe. We simply must find
personal significance, worthy goals, adequate scope, satisfied
intimations—"real life." Of the two main paths to this end,
one is hard packed by the passage of many feet. This classic

western road to our destination has been, especially during the past several hundred years, the broad highway variously called "this-worldliness," "materialism," or "Mammon." America has pre-eminently chosen to follow this route.

The statement implies no accusation. America could hardly have avoided its choice, considering that the nation was born with an endowment of tremendous natural resources, at the time of the Industrial Revolution, and in an era of ascendant individualism. All but inevitably it would put its trust in tangible resources like youth, physical strength, science, bank accounts, insurance. Even when the manifest failure of these items to produce the good life calls forth—as recently—widespread criticism of their real power, America's uneasy faith in assorted externals still remains. We daily continue to breathe an atmosphere of human reliance and blunt materialism, despite our own loud outcry against our "chrome-plated civilization," our secularism, our cult of comfort, our consequent flabbiness in all departments of life.

The present point is that as a result of this familiar environment the western Christian, especially the American Christian, experiences some of the pains of mortification even before he begins its actual practice. Whenever he ponders the advice, "Lay not up for yourselves treasures upon earth" (Matt. 6:19), he does so in the midst of a culture based on a completely opposed premise. The Gospel counsel is un-American. If he actually follows it he knows that he will do so at the certain risk of being painfully different, alone, and misunderstood. We are especially stressing that he will often look askance at himself with his own eyes, not only before the start but also as he travels his lonely road. Those who have tried it can testify that it is not easy to watch one's own generation keep on "going up" in the world while oneself stands still or "goes down." From time to time they wonder, to put the matter mildly. Crass souls begin to doubt our Lord's wisdom. More sensitive ones begin to realize that the desire for sanctity can in itself be a subtle temptation, proceeding from pride. In either case there is apt to be another proof of the sagacity of Chesterton's observation in *What's Wrong with the World*: "The Christian ideal has not been tried and found wanting; it has been found difficult and left untried."

Hypothesis can really become conviction, in this or any living matter, only by dint of continued personal involvement. A "leap of faith" must be made. However, it may help somewhat as we face the difficult decision to fly in the face of majority opinion if we consider deeply the revealing fact that fear is omnipresent in our civilization.

It is a truism that confidence, along with most other really significant human goods, simply cannot be bought with money or legislated by Congress. Only God can give it. The opposite face of this coin proclaims that the cultivation of material reliance is the equal cultivation of fear. Inevitably, therefore, the great modern neurosis is anxiety—and thus, quite pragmatically, our fearful world sufficiently condemns the basis of its own civilization. Unaided by any other consideration—unaided even by the Bomb, which highlights the failure of our success—the terror of our times helps make clear that we have "merely" been going down the wrong road in our search for real life, which banishes fear.

A closely allied pressure, less philosophical and hence more immediate, bears upon every American Christian as he considers the practice of mortification: his daily life is spent in the company of those who are consumed by the manifest compulsion to "strike it rich." Unless he enters a monastery he will be almost irresistibly tempted to conform, because his "have-not" friends freely admit they are Spartan only because of necessity, and are constantly scheming to escape this predicament. Any antimaterialism they voice is a lament at their own lack of material possessions—a deplorable condition which they devoutly trust that application, theft, or Santa Claus will speedily remedy. On the other hand his friends who "have" are delightful people who, if they bewail the secularism of these last days, do so from the depths of foam rubber, between nibbles at fried locusts and cultivated honey, sips of martini, and longing glances at a slick advertisement extolling the irrelevant glamor of the latest necessity.

It is safe to predict that this situation will continue as long as envy and covetousness endure. No editorial hue and cry against materialism can induce any realist to believe that Americans by the disillusioned millions ("Is *that* all there is to life?") will deliberately seek a more Spartan, much less a more otherworldly, mode of existence. Honest observation around one conforms to honest observation within one on this point. The universal spectacle calls to mind a rich young man who was told that in order to follow Christ he would first of all have to sell all and give it to the poor, but who went away in sorrow because of his great possessions. America, which is a very rich young man indeed, does show many signs of being haunted by greater dreams and loftier ambitions than it has achieved in the past, but it too turns away sorrowing, for the identical reason.

Naturalistic commentators on America's material morass seem divided in their opinions as to whether there is any escape from it short of a Republican election, ruinous inflation, national bankruptcy, internal revolution, foreign invasion, or all of these dread cathartics combined. However, the genuine alternative to our becoming one with Babylon, Rome, Nineveh, and Tyre lies where it has always lain since the dawn of history. It lies in the wills of individuals who,

in the always desperately difficult choice between God and
Mammon (God has always been invisible while this world
has always been quite ready to hand), decide to take our Lord
at his word and gamble on God. Neither America nor any
other nation will ever choose mortification as a national
ideal and practice. On the contrary, our present point is that
American people conspire, along with American philosophy, to make the choice of mortification even more painful
than it admittedly is.

More subtly disconcerting as a person debates mortification, the Christian solution to the problem of our amphibian
nature, is the fact that we do live on this earth for a
while, in a body with its physical needs and in a world made
by God for our temporary enjoyment. We know that we live
in a world created by God (not by the Devil, who never created anything real in his life) wherein all things are essentially good and can be legitimately enjoyed. A fearful rejection of good things and an ever more fearful rejection of the
enjoyment of good things are diabolic teachings which have
been exposed thousands of times, only to crop up again because of the insatiable urge of the Father of Lies to have
other created beings become as miserable as he himself is.

The vacillating soul, mindful of "I came that they might
have life, and that they might have it more abundantly"
(John 10:10), realizes that Christianity does not extol the
dour, the joyless, or the reduction of life to subsistence level
and below. He remembers that it was the great apostle of
holy poverty, St Francis himself, who sang the canticles of
the sun, the moon and the stars; the wind, the cloud, and the
air; the fruits and flowers and grass. Above all, he rejoices
that God incarnate entered life so completely that some people who actually saw him, if with limited vision, called him
"a gluttonous man and a winebibber" (Luke 7:34). The dis-

ciple is tremendously aware that Christ enjoyed life's parties, wedding feasts, seaside picnics, dances, fatted calves, and games in the market place far more than the Puritans did or do.

Because of this constant difficulty it bears restating that, in Christian ascetics, mortification is not so much a matter of renunciation as of affirmation. Mortification does not proceed from disgust with this world because this world is bad —which, again, it is not. It aims at disentanglement from this world because, being merely good, it is the enemy of the best. The clarity of Christian insight recognizes that we live in two worlds even now, only one of which is eternal, and hence that it is short-sighted folly to become totally attached to the passing one. "Provincial you might call the soul contented there." As a matter of fact the ripe fruit of mortification, detachment, itself is a means to an end. The end is attachment to God. Thus the practice of mortification does not take us out of life but into Life. We progressively die to one world in order to live progressively in another. Accusations of world weariness, ivory-tower unreality, or cowardly withdrawal all miss the point entirely. Detachment is a right-proportioned objectivity that sees the temporal under the aspect of the eternal.

Furthermore, we must "die in order to live" because of the way we are made. Man's true psychology has never been better stated than in the famous "Thou hast made us for thyself, and the heart is restless until it finds its rest in thee." St Augustine correctly discerned that since we are made for the best, only the best will fulfill us—the best, of course, is God. In his immortal sentence he tells us why millions of things can please us but no thing can content us.

In addition he hints at the reason why millions of things can actually destroy us. The inference is clear that any idolatry of a "less than best" penetrates far deeper than to the level of a temporary restlessness which might be alleviated by turning to a new interest. Continued idolatry must leave us ultimately frustrated (a good description of Hell) because we cannot avoid becoming more and more absorbed into the object of our worship—our perilous glory is that we are constantly becoming what we are. If, for example, we love above all other items that insignificant self of ours we progressively narrow it down toward the vanishing point. If we idolize things, we become increasingly enmeshed in thingness—a miserable, if prevalent, fate. If we exalt people above all other loyalties, we do the human race the worst disservice in the world. It could not be otherwise, given the purpose for which we were made—to know God, to love God, to serve God, and in this only proper worship to become more like him. Everything in the universe is a means to this end. The impoverishment arises when ends and means are confused.

Mortification discerns this. It applies to created things the searching, if not simple, test of whether they minister to or detract from our eternal purpose. Hence in detachment, the fruit of mortification, "I am monarch of all I *survey*," as that qualified expert Thoreau points out. We own, but we are not owned. We enjoy this passing world, yet without any possessiveness toward it. Therefore we are none the poorer when an object of our enjoyment is stolen away from us by the thieving years. Indeed, over those same thieving years, by means of steadily increasing detachment from the things we cannot take with us in the pockets of our shrouds, we enter more and more deeply into the one abiding Attachment.

Our Lord's well-known words on this whole matter appear most succinctly in the familiar sixth chapter of St Matthew's Gospel. The essential point of the passage is that, since we cannot possibly serve both God and Mammon for any extended length of time (one will ultimately crowd the other out, for each has a growing edge, or contagious quality), it is wisdom to hold God in direct vision and Mammon in peripheral vision rather than the other way around. "Be not anxious, saying, What shall we eat—or drink—or wear." The section concludes with the famous statement on life's fundamental choice between God and Mammon: "Seek ye first the kingdom of God and his righteousness; and all these things shall be added unto you."

As we pursue the point that mortification brings painful strain to faith itself, we note that the verse just quoted does not end by saying "and you will have no need of these things." It says we will get them. Millions of people, who have indeed bet their whole lives on this promise, testify that it is perfectly true. They testify additionally, however, to at least three important matters of commentary:

1. More than what is physically needed as we serve God is not promised. In fact, most of the time it is not given. "God is poor pay," as a general rule, for he is not in direct competition with the pay check or Las Vegas. The fact that he does compete, successfully, with every employer in the world in the area of fringe benefits is not widely questioned. The additional truth that he does literally give us what we really need, in the realm of the things which money can buy, finally comes home to the soul after much frantic worrying.

2. We do not always, by any means, get the things we think we need when we think we need them. That "God is slow pay" is usually true—although it must be added that on some special occasions God does provide liberally even before we realize that unusual resources will soon be needed. However, this is his prevenience. The need will come into existence immediately afterward. The usual rule, despite these exceptions, is that our faith is severely tested right up to the very hour. Ultimately—again after much frantic worry—we come to realize that we receive the things we

need in God's good time, which is always our own best hour.

3. Immunity from trial and hardship is not promised. Doubtless one reason we widely misread the promise in this regard, despite the ever-present crucifix which shows the truth of the matter, lies in an archaism of the English language. "Take no thought" about mundane matters is what the King James Version reads. In the common usage of its day the phrase constituted a good translation of the Greek, but of course this is no longer true. "Be not anxious" is a far better modern equivalent. We do have to take a great deal of thought, mingled with enormous effort. The point is that if we "take care of God's business, he will take care of ours."

Strictly speaking, the "practice of mortification" is a contradiction in terms; it is obviously impossible to become attached to detachment. Experience testifies that, practically as well as semantically, God alone provides or permits our real mortifications. The soul itself, however, must work diligently in this field if only to create a sensitive apparatus that can receive intelligibly what God sends.

Initially this practice consists in a really severe and searching series of deaths to this material world. It involves saying "no," quite constantly, to those things which are taking our real riches away from us. To implement this requires a stringent disregard of the appeals of the mere senses—an increasing deafness and blindness to the clamor of the world and the visions of new, shiny, transient things. (Is God deliberately doing us a favor by dulling our physical senses as we grow older?) Ten thousand distracting sense impressions continue to pour in upon us every day, long after they have finished their proper work of bringing us into contact with reality and hence into the beginnings of being. Detachment from the world necessarily involves vigilant mortification of our sensory equipment, to cut off the allurement before it reaches us. "If thine eyes offend thee—" (Matt. 18:9).

Universal application of this elementary principle of Christian ascetics would, of course, force certain adjustments in America's present economy, beginning with Madison Avenue. Has anyone ever seen an advertisement whose appeal was not based on at least one of the seven capital sins? Pressing harder on the writer's share of a group conscience, however, is the knowledge that one of our "eyes"—the Church Militant—presently stands in grave danger of offending most seriously in this area. It is becoming so involved in the world that its trumpet cannot sound without danger of hypocrisy. Any missionary bishop, for example, can testify to the difficulty of inducing young seminarians to come over and help him; there are pleasant curate's jobs in plenty, at a higher salary. The weekly list of "clerical changes" often suggests the same tale.

Naturally there are many other sides to this story, including the fact that some vestrymen are in peril of their souls for grinding the faces of the poor—for causing midnight tears to many a clergyman's wife who cannot see how ends will ever meet. God cannot be solely interested in the sanctification of clergy wives. Yet this sin lies deeper, down among the non-tithing laity who give ample evidence that they have come into the Church solely for what they can derive from it. This is a legitimate beginning, of course, but it is only a beginning. In this area, too, one must be steadily moving towards "the love of God for God." (No experienced pastor can ever forget, however, that the Church does abound, far more than is generally realized, with magnificent people who are not merely moving in the direction of stewardship. They have arrived.)

Conceivably, of course, it could be a dangerous thing for the Church Militant if everyone did tithe, because the

Church empowered has, historically, always fallen upon evil days just like the rest of us. The Church is not exempt from Goldsmith's judgment that "Ill fares the land, to hastening ills a prey, Where wealth accumulates, and men decay." In the millennial state of our imagining, would the Church lavishly give all its resources into the hands of the poor, or would it merely build bigger barns? An Episcopalian is forced to wonder about this, because he knows that the Episcopal Church and its clergy rank close to the top of the "status" list. This is one of the most dreadful indictments of us that could possibly be made.

Leaving this matter of personal speculation we must sketch out the application of mortification to people—that forsaking of father and mother about which our Lord has spoken (e.g. Luke 14:26). Dependence upon people, possessiveness toward people, curiosity about people, exploiting people, seeking people and using people for merely natural gratification, setting people above higher loyalties (or below lesser ones, as for example when compromising principles because of what still other people might think or say)—from all this we must disentangle. No one would argue that statement in theory. In actual practice the parting involves sweet sorrow, particularly in a society inclined to believe wholly the half-truth that real life is based on meeting, reciprocity, and acceptance. Especially if we are influenced by this present fashion in opinions, we will find it exceedingly painful to grow into the likeness of the true servant of God, who more often than not "is despised and rejected of men; a man of sorrows, and acquainted with grief" (Isa. 53:3).

Yet all this external detachment, this building of defenses against the encroachments of the pleasant temporary abode that presses upon us, is only the beginning. Indeed it is true that mere exterior discipline can readily make us worse than we were before—self-righteous, disgruntled, frustrated, hard, sorrowfully martyred. A necessary corrective lies in the internal discipline of thought, imagination, desire, judgment. This process frees these fine instruments to serve their designed ends, instead of permitting their prostitution with the claptrap which so often obsesses them.

It is important to realize that this can be done. We can indeed bring our minds under control, because fortunately our minds can attend to only one thing at a time. St Paul gives us the everlastingly basic advice here—"Whatsoever things are true, honest, just, pure, lovely, of good report— think on these things" (Phil. 4:8). When the mind sets out on other journeys we can, by deliberate effort, practice mental hygiene to the glory of God. In addition we can develop a disciplined mind by the determined practice of mental prayer. We can build up the habit of recollection by making our minds behave as in the presence of God.

All this leads towards the mortification of our desires— those things we think we want and those things we think we fear. The ultimate goal is the absolute "silence" of desire, an unscalable summit that nevertheless we can work toward by increasingly earnest desire for the things that God has in mind for us—"I desire" and "I crave" are bitter curses when the "I" is not united to God. We must begin asking ourselves "What for?" with the greatest possible honesty when we find ourselves thinking "I want." Better, we should in every way cultivate the knowledge of God as a loving and providing Father, who does give us what we need but is not fooled by what we merely want.

Among the most precious things he gives us is aid toward our growing detachment, as that African missionary discerned; for if we really desire what he desires we are well on our way toward that pinnacle of grace which happily accepts what he sends or permits. Our self-examination in this area consists of the question, "What is my response to my today?"—to this job, this interruption, this boring conversation, this humiliation, this uncertainty, this headache, this particular providing of God, who, knowing what I really need, either sends or allows the things of today? Our preference, of course, is for showy crosses in which we can take the greatest pride, but these desires are not crosses, nor will they help us cross over. We must detach from them.

The very mention of "cross" introduces the highest form of God's activity leading us to our death from the merely natural. This is the murky subject of pain and suffering. Since later sections of this book will be concerned with other aspects of this essential mystery, here in connection with mortification we must confine the discussion within narrow limits. It must suffice here to isolate the point that pain is surgery, sent or permitted by God in order to detach us from ourselves—our pride is the only thing about us that can really be hurt—and from the world.

The worldling, quite consistently with his philosophy, either resists pain with all his might, thus adding more pain, all of it non-redemptive, to his situation; or he exploits it, in order to win sympathy for himself and to bind others to his service. On the other hand, that soul is really beginning to be dead to natural values and united to supernatural ones who is discerning, however from afar, that all the pains as well as the pleasures of life are from the hand of God or in the hand of God. When it responds to them as being from the hand of God a great step has been taken in abandoning itself completely into that hand. Mortification, having produced detachment, has begun to allow room for Attachment.

2 Humility

One of the finest fruits of mortification is the great virtue of humility.

In another era such a statement would have strongly supported our thesis that mortification leads to real life rather than pointless death. Nowadays the situation is different. Humility is still recognized as a human value specifically brought to the fore by Christ, but no longer does the word "humility" automatically connote "fullness of life" to us. Hence it seems necessary to point out that the criticism, often amounting to scorn, which is sometimes directed against the virtue of humility, is generally wide of the mark. Its usual, and deserved, target is the pride that apes humility. The rare virtue itself is indeed widely admired when we actually see it exhibited in other people. Most of us like to be in the company of the genuinely humble, for humility is essentially honesty.

Technically considered, humility is the recognition of creatureliness—the cheerful acknowledgment that we are dependent upon our Creator for all things, including that very dependence. Obviously this God-centeredness leaves no room for any annoying human pettiness like self-importance, fanaticism, edginess, anger, boasting. Above all, when it is revealed in human life humility shows itself as a complete unpretentiousness. The humble person adopts no postures. He sees, acknowledges, and accepts himself as being exactly what he is, no more and no less. He is utterly genuine, and interested only in things that are genuine.

It is noteworthy that even the shallowest people often find it quite refreshing and restful to be in the presence of humility. They sense an extra dimension—the dimension of true human greatness as opposed to mere ability. They glimpse overtones of depth and breadth, of vision and patience, of roundness and largeness, which radiate both peace and challenge. Their own uneasy hackles come to rest as for a moment their interest turns towards what *is*, rather than what they are trying to promote. The strong aura of reality that surrounds humility has reached out to them, persuading them to forego for a while the exhausting effort of their own pretendings.

This well-known, if too rare, experience indicates that there is nothing weak in humility. Indeed the contrary is true. Weakness resides in and is of course confessed by the edginess which results in brashness and bluster, whereas the realism that is humility has the solid strength of the everlasting hills. Lincoln and Lee, for example, were humble men. Supremely, so was Jesus. Posers, both among disciples and enemies, often stood in the presence of the honest Christ, without exception to be confounded by him. Sometimes they fell on their knees, saying "Depart from me, for I am a sinful man" (Luke 5:8). At other times they slunk silently away. On occasion he drove them out bodily. In the end, of course, they ganged up on him to achieve a measure of success in the borrowed strength of numbers, but no one of discernment has deduced from this that humility is weakness.

Despite these realizations, even despite our own desire for humility as we become more sick and tired of play acting, it is the hardest of all virtues to acquire. One reason for this inheres in the fact that it is directly opposed to the essential unreality that besets us—pride. In the subtle possessiveness of this pride we perversely feel that humility actually threatens our being instead of constituting its fulfillment. When we stifle this feeling and get down to actual practice the difficulty becomes supreme. The sensitive nerve of pride, which began to quiver when merely looked at, comes into its own when violent hands are laid upon it. Another way of indicating the difficulty of making this basic virtue ours is by pointing out the "circular" nature of humility: to be humble, or honest, or really ourselves is in one sense the end result of a successful life, while in another sense it is the necessary beginning of all progress. Humility, the ending of selfish desires, is only the beginning of desire for what God wants—and when, and how. It is the meeting place of being and becoming.

In addition to this inward difficulty, humility is diametrically opposed to the accepted values of the world around us —values which have soaked so thoroughly into us that we have an ingrained prejudice against the truth. Because we went over this ground in the previous chapter it will suffice here to restate swiftly what we then considered more at length: There are two worlds in which we may freely choose to live—the supernatural world of God's grace or the natural world of man's dis-grace. Unfortunately it often happens that the virtues of one world are not especially valuable in the other. Humility is a classic illustration of this.

To take an example bearing specifically on our present subject, in the natural world of evolution and the survival of the fittest (fitness being defined by those who survive) a certain brashness is a most useful quality. The famous phrase "Nice guys finish last" illustrates this in reverse. One "arrives" through the use of power in discreet or indiscreet ways. A man can discern that he has arrived because he then possesses power, prominence, and the ability to command, however nicely this is done. In the tangible world around us, success and importance are married, or at least keep such steady company that they are almost always found hand in hand. This is notoriously true in our status-conscious society.

The exact opposite, of course, is the case in the supernatural world. It cannot be said too often or too emphatically that humility is the foundation virtue there; that "the greatest among you" is something very different there. Is it too fanciful to suggest that God deliberately began his earthly career in a manger as a tiny baby partly to show us that humility is the beginning from which all else develops? In any case our Lord's undeviating mind on the subject of humility is too well known to need restatement or documentation here. That he was, of course, absolutely correct in considering humility the foundation-stone of the spiritual building is clearly revealed by the pragmatic evidence of his earthly ministry, in its successes and in its failures. He succeeded with the humble; he failed with the proud. Thus it has always been in the story of religion, both before and after Christ. To twist a familiar phrase from the First Epistle to St Peter, God simply cannot give his grace except to the humble who will not resist the gift (cf. I Pet. 5:5).

To take another example of these opposed values, most of us hail the Renaissance as a heaven-sent forward movement of the human spirit, when the world after its long Dark Ages became man-centered instead of God-centered. Religion views the matter differently. Of course no one denies the numerous particular blessings that stem from the Renaissance;

all of us use many of them daily, quite gladly and quite prop-
erly. However, in the religious view of life, to become man
centered instead of God centered is the essentially ruinous
human situation. The exaltation of man, the exaltation of
self, is precisely original sin—the very principle of disorder
which sets all creation jangling. In the Church's mythology
it was the Devil who said to Adam and Eve, "Eat, and be as
God" (cf. Gen. 3:5).

The Church's insistence that this humanism can only be
a disastrous philosophy, because it puts things exactly backwards, is amply borne out by history. The most observable
fact of our own day is that centuries of making the will of
man the be-all and the end-all have brought us to the very
point where tomorrow could easily be the end-all. However,
we do not need the newspaper to testify afresh each morning that if man is indeed the measure of all things then things
are in bad shape. The pathetic and horrible story of the human race, blithely pursuing its own way both before and
after the Renaissance, clearly reveals us to be so petty and
vicious that we are hardly worth blowing up—although in
our cynical moments that seems an excellent idea.

To take still another example of the opposed value sys-
tems, consider the widely prevalent teaching (often in the
name of psychology and religion) that bids us feed our egos
on this and on that, for our souls' health. The saints' contrary
claim, down through the ages, is that we can only rightly
feed our egos on God. They say that we can only become ourselves when full of God, not when full of self. In this they
find themselves completely in agreement with Christ, who
pointed out on many an occasion that when we are choked
to the brim with the "cares and riches and pleasures of this
life" (Luke 8:14), there is no room whatsoever for God.

These illustrations hardly sketch the fundamental opposition, yet they may faintly indicate the searing travail which

awaits the soul who really sets out in pursuit of humility, defying both his inner inclinations and his outer environment. The great virtue will be gradually acquired, however, by making spiritual use of precisely these opposed forces. Brief illustration of this process will be sufficient here, for once again we are on ground covered in the previous chapter.

Enormous raw material for growth in humility is ready to hand in our temptations. The self-made man reacts with irritation when his weak spots are thus sought out; in the same experience a spiritual person relearns the depths of his own incapacities for good. He uses the constant proof of his potential sinfulness to lead him into deepening dependence upon God—"there, but for the grace of God, go I." Perhaps from time to time he rejoices in the thought that the Devil must be experiencing great despair at having his best assaults thus turned to his own confusion.

Another unfailing flow of opportunity to grow in humility is found in humiliation itself. An ample inner supply of this is always available in our sins and (perhaps not so often, for we are clever at concealment) in the humiliation of being discovered in them. Incidentally, an unfailing test of growing humility is found in our reaction to criticism. If our first impulse is to feel that our critic is probably right, we have come a long way.

In this connection it is well to point out that the only humiliation we should deliberately seek is the humiliation of the confessional; the search for humiliation on all other occasions is born of pride. Seeking out humiliation is usually quite unnecessary. It is sufficient in our fallen world that we accept with all grace the humiliations which the world flings our way. The entire armor of a sinful, stupid, and unjust environment—misunderstandings, misquotations, slanders, failures—which makes the natural man red faced, disappointed, discouraged, or even despairing, is the finest kind of material for learning humility, when rightly used.

Temptation and humiliation are, as it were, steady daily teachers in the school of humility. In addition, on occasion a visiting examiner comes to test our progress. Every life has its critical moments, when we know with special clarity that we do not dare trust our own strength. There are times—as when we face a serious operation, or undertake a new job, or watch our business fail, or in any way become lost in the woods—when the whole human and cosmic affair is too big for us. We are adrift on a tiny raft in the middle of a boundless ocean. In this situation, when a person is thrown back upon really basic resources, he can easily be reckless or despairing in a hundred different ways. On the other hand, profiting from the experience, he can learn a deeper degree of dependence on the strength of God.

These three factors—temptation, humiliation, crisis—that come our way in the providence of God or the maliciousness of events provide the most excellent material for growth in humility. Our own cooperating life of prayer as we grope toward the virtue is the final factor that will be mentioned here.

It has already been hinted that humility does not originate in our squashing ourselves down. Such self-abasement is born of pride. True humility, on the contrary, comes through magnifying God. (Indeed, everything that can be said on our subject is in commentary on the Magnificat.) It is born and flourishes as a by-product of the cultivated habit of looking up and away from oneself. A mountain range, the endless ocean, the sweep of stars at night—contemplation of these things often helps the viewer see his true size. In the same manner the prayer of adoration—von Hügel has shown us that the essential religious attitude is adoration—recognizes the centrality of God and the peripheral location of the adorer. We have seen that this right proportion is the essence of humility.

It follows that the prayers of praise and thanksgiving, the attitudes of worship and adoration, are the fundamental ones which must be the ever-growing elements in our total prayer life. As through deliberate cultivation they come to bulk larger and larger in our life of prayer, the growing knowledge of our own creatureliness will slip in from the side.

Our preparation for Holy Communion, in which supreme spiritual activity we receive into our nothingness him who is everything, provides a perfect illustration here. There are many ways to prepare for Holy Communion, but all real preparation consists in setting oneself aside so that God may be all. Any real communicant knows he needs God, and that in Holy Communion he receives God. In preparation he strives to drop himself and to desire God.

This striving is the cultivation of what is dangerously called "holy indifference," which is not so much a passive as an active desire for God's will. Holy indifference desires what God desires, in his time and manner. It doesn't care whether one is president or janitor, so long as that is what God wants. It doesn't care whether life is lived in exhilaration or deadness, by flashing inspiration or dry duty, so long as that is what God wants at the moment.

The essence of the matter is that holy indifference doesn't fuss about itself, but attends to God. Indeed it does not so much fight self, or argue with self, as merely drop self as being of no particular consequence in comparison with God—yet as being safely in the hands of God. This is the morning that dawns at the end of the night of humility.

We have been stressing the fact that our growing awareness of God as our almighty Creator and loving Father brings, with equal strides, the happy knowledge of our creaturehood and sonship. This can be expressed in more living terms by saying that a person has really begun to be religious who knows that God at all times has given him what is best for him, is doing so now, and will continue to do so. He is discovering the astonishing truth that the will of God is always good—and good for him. In addition, he has begun to see that the worldly definition of success has a bad habit of missing the point entirely. This is partly because it judges between person and person as if they had the same needs and responded equally to the same situations (which they don't) but mainly because prominence, prestige, position, and a sound bank balance are not the ultimate sources of security. As he perseveres on this course he will approach the time when he is not much bothered by insecurity at all, because in desiring solely the will of God he is finding the only security there is.

3 Temptation

To class temptation among the specific desolations of the advancing spiritual life may seem at first glance to involve some straining. Surely everybody, including the avowedly irreligious person, experiences temptation. And what low degree of meaning are we putting on the word "desolations"?

While fuller replies to these objections will develop as this chapter progresses, it can immediately be stated, quite flatly, that the natural man really knows almost nothing about temptation. He succumbs so readily to the unsophisticated wiles of the third-rate tempter who is practicing on him that he never comes in contact with anything really significant or subtle. The world itself acknowledges in various ways the truth of this assertion. There is, for example, its pathetic witticism "I can resist anything except temptation." There is the fact that its respected leaders fall easy prey to self-evident matters of morality like price fixing. There is its naïve conviction that sin is pretty well limited to gross physical matters like murder and the theft of large sums.

Consideration of the second objection, which will lead back to and further document our initial dogmatism, starts with the reminder that this book is concerned to expose certain elements that conspire to weaken, or stop altogether, the spiritual effort. A matter of practical experience among spiritual directors is that inadequate knowledge of the facts about temptation is high among these deterrents.

One great reason for this is that, quite characteristically, the beginner in the spiritual life tends to think that his temptations will soon be outgrown. Indeed, he may well have "tried God" in a last desperate hope that this endeavor may smooth out his life for him. He consults his pastor, under his guidance adopts a rule of life, and gladly pursues it in eager anticipation of the consummation when—after a couple of months of diligent effort, to take a long view of the matter— he will be an integrated personality in full possession of his perfected nature. His present temptations will then surely be gone or at least under such splendid control that they will present no real problem.

Of course that happy time never comes. So, to counteract disenchantment, the facts of the matter should be made clear at the outset. The facts are that the greatest saints universally testify that they are the most tempted, rather than the least tempted, of human beings.

This is true for many reasons, of which the one closest to our purpose is that as we journey on the spiritual road we are penetrating ever more deeply into enemy territory. Each bit of progress brings us closer to the big guns, which our adversary turns against us in increasingly powerful and desolating ways. To turn this figure around a bit, as we grow stronger and more fit for the spiritual combat God puts us into the front lines where the warfare is harder. The Church Militant is at war against the evil around us, as well as against the evil within us. After our basic training, God does us the honor of using us in this battle. It is recorded of Father Benson of Cowley that he replied to the evangelist's question,

"Brother, have you found peace?" by firmly declaring "No. War!"

The encouraging corollary involved in the point we are urging is that when we are hard pressed we are pressing harder; pressure is always reciprocal. The persistence of temptation and the increase of temptation, far from indicating failure, indicate rather our own spiritual growth. Perhaps for this reason, in addition to the one he states, St James wrote "Count it all joy when ye fall into divers temptations" (Jas. 1:2). Certainly the testing means that we are making progress. The Devil would not take us so seriously unless we constituted a real threat to his purposes. God would not yet trust us in a vital matter unless he knew we were ready for the test.

In short, temptation is annoying, wearying, constant, and—as we persevere—increasing, but it is not a negative or useless element. Nor is it, like a sand fly at a picnic, an intruding interruption into the otherwise good life. Temptation is of the everlasting nature of things. It obviously existed even before the fall of man; indeed it was the inciting cause of that disaster. Human freedom is real, even in a state of grace, as Adam and Eve discovered to our sorrow. Temptation is merely harder to fight, now that we are weaker.

Obviously we need every aid in its perpetual and increasing conflict, but before considering some of the particular weapons of that warfare it is encouraging to note that the battle is not merely defensive, or wearily negative. There is great positive good in temptation—the goods, for example, which proceed from its being a test of character and reality. The chapter on humility noted that the strength of temptation helps to deepen humility and fortify our desire to cling to God. Gifted as we are in self-delusion, we would surely imagine ourselves masters of every virtue unless temptation sought us out to warn us of our weaknesses and to caution us against pride. The outgoing, affirmative side of this truth is that temptations are a constant spur to definite spiritual effort—consequently to definite spiritual progress—because they remind us daily that we cannot drift. Struggle is necessary, we know. Heaven is taken by storm, we have read. Temptation provides the moral exercise, against strong opposition, that prevents our becoming flabby. Genuine people would not want to be without it, because lacking it they would be living without creative tension. They are well aware that those overlauded spiritual states, peace of mind and peace of soul, do not in the least resemble the bucolic placidity of the cow chewing its cud in a meadow.

The nature of temptation must be analyzed (we shall follow Father Harton closely in this) if only for one reason: Everyone knows that temptation is not sin—"Yield not to temptation, for yielding is sin"—yet most of us know this only intellectually. When actually involved in personal battle, however, there is tremendous pressure on a sensitive soul to believe he has fallen into the most desolating sin when, in actual fact, he has won a significant victory. He has indeed been strongly tempted, but he has resisted the temptation completely.

The first stage in temptation is suggestion, or awareness, proceeding from one of our three enemies. (It is comforting to realize that our enemies are indeed only three in number—the world, the flesh, and the Devil—rather than the legion we are apt to imagine.) Somehow, through the imagination, the appetite, the eyes, the mind, we become aware of a possibility.

We repeat that this is merely the way things are in the world of human free will. The fact reflects our glory rather than our fault.

Blame does not accompany the second stage of temptation,

either—our enjoying it. This is the point, however, at which many of us tend to become confused, especially as we develop spiritually. The obvious truth is that temptation *has* to suggest advantages or be pleasant. Lacking this appeal there would be no temptation. This point is so important, however, and so easily overlooked in the heat of battle, that it must be underlined.

The most evil suggestions and desires, even when responded to with speed and delight from the recesses of our Freudian depths, are not sin. They are not sins, they remain only temptations, until we say a deliberate "yes." They can strongly beset us for the most protracted periods—they can even last all of our life, as St Francis de Sales points out—with no harm at all being done. Indeed, it is useful and comforting to remember that the stronger any temptation grows the more we are resisting it. This is one of the reasons why the saints are not only the most tempted, but also the most strongly tempted. They don't give up supinely at the first suggestion, but fight on to the end. From this point of view alone our Lord himself, who was "in all points tempted like as we are, yet without sin" (Heb. 4:15), was the most severely tempted of all who ever shared the human lot.

The final stage, the bridge between temptation and sin, is the consent of the will. This is ours to control; neither God nor the Devil can force it. Thus we have arrived at the point where it is necessary to sketch out some weapons in the resisting of temptation.

In the forefront of these is a basic theological and spiritual awareness that God is our loving Father. It is the greatest source of strength to know this, and hence to know that in permitting temptations he will definitely not allow us to be assailed by those that are too strong for us at our present stage of development. Moral theology, in its chilly way, expresses the beginnings of this point in the true distinction between material and formal sin—if conscience is not yet

sensitive in an area, the soul may freely trespass there without personal guilt. "Ignorance of the law" is, with God, indeed an excuse. Hence the beginner blunders blindly, yet
safely, through fields which the sensitive spiritual eye sees
to be strewn with land mines.

A higher level of the subject is expressed in St Paul's assurance that "God is faithful, who will not suffer you to be
tempted above that ye are able" (1 Cor. 10:13). This aspect of the enormous fact of God's providence is in line with
our Lord's implication that God, the Father of man and
sparrow, will not push a bird out of its nest before it can fly.
Of course he will when it can, which may well be long before
it thinks it can. Hence whenever we fear we are being tried
too hard, the truth is that we are either stronger than we
think or (what is more probable) we are neglecting the
means of grace. The everlasting point is that God knows our
state. Even in the loneliness of our severest trials God is loving us, trusting us, aiding us, and leading us to greater
strength through that trial. The human spirit, throughout
history, expresses itself on this theme with one confident voice
of infinite variety—now in the hymn "How firm a foundation," again in Francis Thompson's *The Hound of Heaven*,
perhaps supremely in the 23rd Psalm. Who has not responded
with his own fervent "Amen"?

This assurance most not lead us to presumption. Presumption in the spiritual life makes the fundamental error
of considering it too simple a thing to serve God. While God
is, of course, quite easy to please he is terribly hard to satisfy.
Presumption corrupts the idea of God's tremendous attributes—love, mercy, forgiveness, providence, fatherhood—
into a mere amiable good nature. The Old Testament conception of "Father" lay in the mind of our Lord when he
used that title. "Father" is, indeed, his only title for God,
but the Old Testament overtones in the word are not the
watered-down American ones. In Hebraic usage the word

always connotes, among other things, authority of a sovereign nature. The Hebrew father was "the centre from which strength and will emanate to the whole group which belongs to him," to quote Kenneth Grayston.

Presumption corrupts this, substituting an idea of God that is closer to that of Santa Claus. In so doing it adds injury to insult by making a mockery of human dignity. To be human, made in the image and likeness of God, is no light matter. As Grayston points out, "a son is one who not only acknowledges the father's authority, but also bears his character." In addition, the sons of God enjoy the privilege of working out their own salvation with fear and trembling (Phil. 2:12).

In our weak, sick, or tired moments we may incline to wish we could merely drift along and in the drifting arrive at a worth-while destination. In our better moments, however, we do not want life to be something that happens to us, as it were. We are glad, then, that life is man sized to the point where it requires more than our best efforts. We are galvanized by a call to "blood, tears, toil, and sweat" because we know that these adornments are really quite becoming to humans. They reveal, among other things, our dignity and our worth. Everybody respects people who say, and mean, that they won't ask God to do for them what they can do for themselves.

One of the things we can do about temptations is to keep out of their way—they will seek and find us often enough without being sought after. We must avoid our known occasions of sin whenever possible. These are the circumstances, the places, the people, the idleness, the luxury, and all the other externals which experience has taught us involve "asking for trouble." They also include such dangerous inner company as daydreaming, wishful thinking, hating, envying, coveting.

Again we bear down on a point, because of its importance.

Glibly we pray "lead us not into temptation" and then, often merely in fear of being thought odd by our friends of this earth, we rush out to embrace it. Thus it is that all too often, when a person in a spiritual dilemma plaintively asks "What would our Lord do in these circumstances?" the only completely honest reply is "He wouldn't have got himself into those circumstances"—not an immediately helpful, if true, observation. The point, we are repeating, is that we must not ask for trouble. Trouble, in the schoolboy's delightful definition, is "that thing we can *always* find by looking for it."

This is a practical application of part of our Lord's advice on our subject when, in the garden of Gethsemane, he urged his disciples to "watch and pray" lest they enter into temptation. If we "watch" we will not always be taken by surprise. We will be expecting that, say, in youth the temptations of the flesh will always be lurking just around the corner. We will be expecting that in middle life the temptations of the world—perhaps of overweening ambition, which is a characteristic sin of the mature years—will lie in wait for us. In our last decades on earth we will be expecting the direct attentions of the Devil himself—spiritual temptation like covetousness, that clinging on to what used to be, which is a great and typical danger to the aged.

Speed in dealing with temptation is the next important point—immediacy, not "all deliberate speed." Our Lord himself, in that interpretation of his inner life which is the temptation story recorded in the first and third Gospels (Matt. 4:1-11; Luke 4:1-13), dealt immediately with the flesh, the world, and the Devil as in turn they assailed him. If God incarnate did not toy with the presumption and the partial consent that are involved in dabbling with this matter, how much less can we afford to? We must grasp the nettle firmly, and grasp it immediately.

In certain situations we must run from it immediately. Immediate flight, either through removing our body's pres-

ence or our mind's attention, is the wise course in cases of
emotional temptations. The longer and harder we fight an
emotional temptation, such as sex or hatred or morbid anxiety, on its own ground and while staring it in the face, the
stronger it becomes. Flight from emotional temptation is not
cowardice, but bravery and wisdom.

The other part of our Lord's advice—prayer in temptation—is twofold in its application. There must be, first of
all, a strong background of habitual prayer antecedent to
particular temptation. Indeed, the whole spiritual life is one
of creating good habits to replace bad habits or no habits—a
virtue is "merely" a deliberately cultivated habit. In this
immediate connection it is obvious that we must practice a
regular, habitual, prayer life—indeed, spiritual life in the
broadest sense—if only because temptation is regular. Neglect is the grossest presumption.

Habitual prayer leads us to turn spontaneously to "actual"
prayer as a defensive-offensive weapon when temptation itself comes along. Often this is extremely difficult to do, because the Devil is quick to insinuate two additional temptations. To those who lack the habit of prayer he suggests that
this is an unworthy time to begin begging; to all he points
out that we are not worthy to pray. The strength of this latter
sophistry is increased if he can induce a sensitive victim to
believe that he is soiled by the filth of sin rather than by the
clean sweat of spiritual combat.

The truth of the matter is that we are indeed unworthy
to pray, in temptation or at any other time, but in the love
of God we have an invitation to "come as we are," particularly if we need help. In personal illustration of this fundamental Christian truth, I vividly remember the day our child
disobeyed, climbed a forbidden tree, and ran into a hornets'
nest—a literal one. We parents engaged in no moralistic
debates, at the moment or later. When we heard the an-

guished screams we did exactly what any parents would do in the circumstances, and what God does when his children call. We brought our best swift aid and comfort, as God does when invoked in words, or by the sign of the cross traced on the forehead, or through any other form of actual prayer.

"Watching and praying" in temptation can be linked together by the practice of looking at God rather than staring at the temptation. That is to say, we should make much of the grace needed to resist the onslaught, rather than make much of the temptation. We should turn from it, toward the sources of help against it—as Alcoholics Anonymous so rightly instructs its members. Temptation, when argued with, has its ego flattered and gains strength from the attention. While this is notoriously true in the case of emotional temptations, it is by no means limited to that area. A sad truth, familiar to all, is that the human mind can rationalize absolutely anything at all if it applies itself to the problem diligently enough.

Finally, what if we fail? What if the temptation wins? It is important that we then do not become discouraged—which is a new temptation, often worse than the first. After sin, if failure is to do the good of failure, the penitent and humble soul's dialogue with himself will take this form: "What did I really expect, knowing the kind of person I am? Once again I have learned how badly I stand in need of discipline and grace. I have failed God, but he has not failed me. I will hold all the more firmly to him in the future. I will not continue to sit here nursing my hurt pride, in the delusion that I am a greater sinner than God is a forgiver. I will arise and go to my Father, and say—."

The penitent and humble soul makes an immediate act of contrition, perhaps records the incident for future confession at the regular time and in the regular way, refuses to look back morbidly, and gets up to go on—in sure and certain knowledge that "a saint is a sinner who kept on trying."

4 Aridity

Thus far our main attention has been given to pressures that bear on the soul from outside—to spiritual distress caused by our secular environment, for example. We now begin turning inward by examining, more systematically than in the Introduction, the universal spiritual experience called aridity. That bleak and desert word is apt. So is Harald Tandrup's wry phrase in *Reluctant Prophet*, when after a blunt order to Jonah "the Lord went into his eternity and closed the door behind him."

It has already been indicated that this familiar experience recurs. Not once, but many times, we know the silence of God—an aloofness in God which is far more cutting than the "non-existence" of God. Some of these times coincide with our moments of greatest need, as when "Saul saw the host of the Philistines . . . and his heart greatly trembled." With Saul we cry aloud to heaven, but nothing happens: "And when Saul inquired of the Lord, the Lord answered him not, neither by dreams, nor by Urim, nor by prophets" (1 Sam. 28:5,6). Our prayer has hit a lead shield just in front of us and drops heavily to the ground. We sympathize com-

48

pletely with the woman of Canaan who "came and cried unto
him, saying, Have mercy on me, O Lord, thou son of David;
my daughter is grievously vexed with a devil. But he answered her not a word" (Matt. 15:22,23).

In sober analysis, which doesn't tend to cheer us greatly
when we are actually in a state of spiritual drabness, the
absence of God is caused by (1) the laws of nature, (2) certain elements in ourselves, (3) diabolic activity, (4) certain
facts in God himself.

1. It is of the utmost importance to realize that the experience of aridity is a perfectly natural thing from time to
time, in obedience to well-known laws of human psychology.
Whether we like it or not we are all manic-depressives; some
of us are merely more so than others. There is an ebb and
flow of awareness, of intensity and torpor, of good and bad
moods, which runs through human make-up. If today we
are confident of our ability to conquer the world, two weeks
hence we will be pessimistic, gloomy, and prone to fear.

Since this is true of human nature itself, it is supremely
true in the spiritual life which takes its moment-by-moment
tone from the way the whole self is at the time. Naturally we
are the same people in our religious life as we are in the rest
of our life. So when God is sleeping, when the Church is
futile, when prayers are unreal, when nothing is right, the
first part of wisdom is to wait a few days. The chances are
good that one is merely in the "down" trough of a psychological fluctuation.

Closely connected to this law of our being is the added
psychological fact that a period of reaction follows a period
of sustained application or intense insight. Withdrawal and
return, in large and small degrees, characterize human life.
Indeed, this ebb and flow is structural to all of creation—
winter follows summer, the moon waxes and wanes, the tides
roll in and out, all through nature and every part of nature.

We human beings have not merely been set on a pulsating stage where we have to keep our balance as we act out the play; we pulsate along with the floor and the scenery because (the figure of speech is impossible) we were born of that floor and that scenery.

While it is not necessary to hammer the familiar truth that there are, in the nature of things, these recurrent periods of luxuriant creativity and of lying dormant, experience indicates the necessity of pointing out that this law applies supremely to that most delicate entity, the spiritual life. Far from being surprised by recurrent deadness, we should realize that it is entirely normal. The realization will help us be content to wait. Surprise and suspicion would arise if, indeed, our spiritual nature were the only stable element in the universe.

Equally important is the realization that, graphically speaking, the "line of true growth"—above and below which our fluctuations rise and fall—angles upward from the horizontal. Hence we must not by any means expect to come back to the same level of experience, or to the same delight in that experience, that we knew once long ago. In many ways we "can't go home again" because we are involved in a far more important journey toward our really permanent home. We gladly accept this fact in most secular matters—in childhood we happily cut out paper dolls; now it pleases us more to cut out coupons. The same progression is true in the life of the spirit. We should expect to outgrow certain spiritual practices, just as we outgrow everything else. We should expect to be "surprised by joy" in new ways as our spiritual life deepens, broadens, and—perhaps above all—simplifies. Spiritual covetousness is only one form, if a rather subtle one, of that particular capital sin.

2. However, if one waits until vitality begins to return and still "nothing happens," old or new, the time has come to

examine oneself in order to see if there are contributing causes which can be eradicated. Leaving medical and psychological examination unmentioned, as we must in this book, the first area of this search is for serious sin in thought, word, attitude, deed, and omission. "Mortal" sin does indeed live up to its name by killing the life of God in our souls. Through it, as it were, one gets out of touch with him because one has grieved the Holy Spirit of God and driven him away. The result is, to put it mildly, flatness. One has dropped back to the merely natural level, wherein one lacks the true human wholeness that is only possible when the grace of God is flowing strongly through. The victim of long-continued rejection will of course make sincere confession if he finds that sin stands between him and God. He will be well advised to offer his contrition in any case. Experience testifies that, as a result, he may sense anew that "peace of God" which is one of many proofs that "confession is good for the soul."

Mortal sin, however, is far from being the only cause of God's absence from us "through our own most grievous fault." Especially among advancing souls, loss of fervor finds a more common source in sheer attrition. Just as warm human friendship cools over the years through neglect— through failure to write letters or to telephone; through increasing absorption in new interests—so does our friendship with God. This is not because he becomes "distant" in the social sense of that word, but because our receiving apparatus is tuned to a different wave length. His still small voice is being drowned in static. We are beginning to reinvolve ourselves in the world, here a little and there a little. We have begun to neglect our spiritual life, here a little and there a little. The dust is settling on the mirror of our soul, we are not wiping it away, hence it is not reflecting the Light around it. The Light is as bright as ever, needless to say.

The following illustrations which occur naturally to an Episcopalian can easily be translated into any reader's familiar devotional terms: If I really pray two or three times each day; if I do some spiritual reading daily; if I unfailingly make my daily meditation; if I share in offering the Holy Eucharist twice a week; if I make a spiritual communion each morning and a really prepared sacramental communion weekly; if I engage in some well-loved optional devotion monthly; if I make an annual Retreat; the chances are good that spiritual dryness will not assail me too often—or that, if it assaults, it will yield to this contrary assault. In short, we must keep up our interest. We can lose interest in anything at all by the simple process of failing to make regular deposits. The civic clubs, acting on this principle, wisely insist upon weekly attendance at their session, whether the member feels like it or not.

We can never be too careful that we are going on, always, with our normal spiritual rule. It is—literally—devilishly easy to slip into the absurd opposite; to think: When I feel worthy I will go to Holy Communion; When I feel penitent I will confess my sins; When my spirit is soaring I will pray. How we are taken in by the most ridiculous blandishments of the Father of Lies! Only after morning dawns will we turn on the lights? The true Word has spoken about this matter: "They that be whole need not a physician, but they that are sick" (Matt. 9:12).

3. The Devil's activity in this matter of aridity is not confined to the manner suggested in the paragraph above. To cite a personal illustration at the other extreme, I well remember the saintly old lady who was visited by Satan himself almost daily. Because the flesh and the world had long since lost all power over her, and presumably because lesser demons were completely baffled, he gave her his personal attention. Always a most formidable opponent, in this situation

he was doing his vicious best to scare an old saint to death
with black visions, abysmal despairs, horrid fears of eternal
damnation, and all the other tricks of his trade. The doctors,
quite understandably, attributed it all to hardening of the
arteries, but I am certain that they were very far from being
wholly right.

I brought her Communion twice a week, after which we
would talk. In these conversations I learned a great deal. To
mention only one thing, it was from this lady that I learned
the real meaning and power of Confirmation. She told me
that when his satanic Majesty tormented her she would say,
"I have been confirmed. God the Holy Ghost lives in me.
God is about me, and in me, with full power. What then can
distress me?"

This faithful reliance upon God is always our best weapon
against the Devil. In addition we should remember that he
has at least two weaknesses: he cannot love, and he cannot
laugh. So, while tracing the sign of the cross or throwing holy
water on the sizzling visitor, laugh at him. He will depart, unfortunately only for a season. In his certain return, also
unfortunately, he will be full of great wrath.

4. Certain truths about God himself, which involve his
ways of dealing with us, are the ultimate considerations in
any discussion of the periodic nature of the spiritual life.
God is personal. He moves toward us, or withdraws from
us, somewhat like other persons in their relations with us.
On one occasion the eternal Christ of St John's tremendous
Gospel—a Gospel perhaps especially written for mature
Christians—said quite definitely to his disciples, "A little
while and ye shall not see me; and again a little while and
ye shall see me" (John 16:16). The testimony of the saints
and mystics is that this specific warning can safely be uni-
versalized.

It follows that when no fault, no sin, no lapsing vigor in

our spiritual effort, and no Devil is discerned by honest investigation, God's absence should be left up to God, without any worry, fuss, or other self-regarding elements. "We should never want to please God otherwise than as he pleases to be pleased." Spiritual dryness, if that is his will at the moment, is as much to be loved and obeyed as spiritual fervor. Neither one matters more than the other, except that his loving absence is often a sign of higher favor—it suggests his confidence that we will continue to stand firm without reward. In either case, as in all situations, "thy will be done, not mine."

Of course God, who has sound reasons for all his actions, is not arbitrary or capricious in this matter. For the most part his goings and comings are the way of a non-possessive parent with his child. Our Introduction indicated that God, who is concerned above all that we grow up into him, first surrounds us with a love so sure that we can feel it. After he has thus given us a basic security, from time to time he sends us out on our own. He withholds the props so that we will learn to stand alone, and so increase in strength and the "independence" of real spiritual maturity.

It is a maxim that no parent, including God, can pamper his child if the youngster is to develop. No parent can always do the things that the child likes, or understands, or to which his emotions respond favorably. Indeed, it is not our emotional response but our character, our will, our purpose that is basic. Aridity tempers this as no other fire can.

Once again, God values our best self. He is not interested in puppets, but in people. We have heroic possibilities that are greater than we ourselves know or even want, and God will not compromise with our incessant desire for mediocrity. As we have seen, he strengthens us with crosses, without which no soul has ever reached the heights. His silence, so welcome to the worldling, is one of the severest crosses he sends to those who love to hear his voice.

Finally, we should make it most clear to ourselves that it is God's love for us, rather than our own subjective affection for him, which both assures our salvation and constitutes our eternal joy. We all give lip service to this truth that God, rather than ourselves, is at the center. We profess that human sanctity finds its only solid foundation in God's being, love, and activity. It takes repeated aridity, however, to bring home to us that our own so precious feelings contribute nothing to our salvation; that, in fact, they generally stand in the way of our perfection. Spiritual dryness can finally lead us, after much pouting, actually to give thanks that it is not because we see God that we have joy. It is because he sees us.

Of course, some day when our spiritual cataracts have been removed we shall see him in the eternal joy of the beatific vision. One slight indication of the unarguable fact that we humans are more really at home in eternity than in time is glimpsed here. In longing impatience we crave to leap at the end, disregarding all the necessary means. Yet the ending, together with the beginning and the continuing, is not in ourselves. It is in God, who sees us all the time from his eternity. Even through our present darkness he sees us fully. After he has drawn us closer to himself through that darkness we shall see him again, this time far more distinctly. Meanwhile, in any arid time we can be very sure that some day our joy will return—which means that he who is our joy will return. There is all the difference in the world between our Joy and our subjective joy. Indeed, it is only when he, not ourself, is our joy that our joy can ever be full.

5 Divisions

Everyone, saint and sinner alike, knows that the lawful father of divisiveness, both around us in the social group and within our own split personalities, is the Prince of Darkness. He delights in shredding an individual into tiny clashing pieces and in setting people against one another. He labors fiendishly to produce that Hell, both on this earth and after this earth, in which people keep getting farther and farther apart.

On the other hand, it is common knowledge that the work of God the Holy Ghost is to make cosmos out of chaos, both in the universe and in the individual. On Whitsunday, for example, the Holy Spirit vastly empowered his work of counteracting the divisiveness let loose at the Tower of Babel. A consequent major task of those in whom he lives is to endeavor "to keep the unity of the Spirit in the bond of peace" (Eph. 4:3).

An ever-deepening awareness of the ultimate importance of unity and harmony poses a serious difficulty to advancing souls, for precisely as they are growing in this knowledge they are finding themselves increasingly at variance with the world, with its standards, with its people. Consequently they begin to be puzzled, at the very least. The more sensitive begin to experience exquisite torture. Surely it was, in part, to comfort them that our Lord said such things as "I came to set a man at variance with his brother"—"I came not to bring peace, but a sword"—"I will set the sons against their fathers"—"Blessed are ye when men shall revile you"—all of which sayings St John sums up in his telling phrase, "There was a division among the people *because of him*" (Matt. 10:34-6; 5:11; John 7:43, cf. 9:16, 10:19).

Our Lord was right, of course; division can and does arise because of good, not merely because of evil. Consider the situation within ourselves which memory reminds us was sufficiently chaotic at the start of our spiritual life. Our initial equipment included a great deal of good, mingled with a host of bad habits, many inferior associations, strong attraction to low standards. In addition, the fallen human being whom we then placed in God's hands was not really a self at all, but many conflicting selves all struggling to be dominant.

Under God's hands this initial confusion can readily seem to become even worse for a time. Naturally God gladly came to us just as we were, but he was not content merely to "pull us together." He began, also, to lead us higher. Even conceding that part of our self responded with alacrity, the greater part resisted mightily. We *liked* some of our habits, some of our associations, some of our standards. We were quite certain, in fact, that many of these items were not accidental matters but were actually inseparable components of the sacred me. "Take this away and I won't be me any more" —a cosmic loss, it goes without saying. So we followed God reluctantly, muttering from afar "If you think I'm going to sacrifice *that*—!"

If God overheard he gave no sign. "With unperturbed pace" he continued with his work of draining our swamps and cultivating our highlands. Hence, for a time, he continued to create divisions within us.

These divisions are good, of course. The inner tension is a growing pain, indicating that we are making progress toward becoming ourselves on levels undreamed of before. The attendant frustration helps us to recognize those elements within us which still need either eradication or integration into the real self. Frustration, put to use, serves as a magnifying glass. For example, it helps us discern what is happening when we say, most emphatically, "Now *there's* something that I will never do," whereupon we shortly proceed to do that very thing. The overcompensating "never" reveals, even to ourselves, emergent knowledge of an unworthy element in our character that must yield to higher values. Naturally God, who knows this weak spot too, has exposed it in order to bring about its cure. Soon he leads us to face that particular barrier to growth; we climb over it or batter it down; we enter a larger field; and at last there is one less division within us.

It is extremely important to note, as we discuss divisions, that this same growth process is going on in our neighbor. God is gradually cleansing his temple too; is slowly sanctifying him also, bit by bit. If we may make the unlikely assumption that our neighbor is a more difficult case than we ourselves are, it will follow that at a given moment we can be on a higher level than he is. There are, indeed, nearly infinite levels or stages in spiritual growth (with each individual being different to begin and end with, too) so that the unfortunate person who does not yet see what we perceive is under terrible pressure to argue with us. In our haughty inclination to suspect that we are in full possession of cosmic wisdom, we are under even greater pressure to put the benighted fellow straight. Great grace is necessary, both in the self-appointed saint and in his intended victim—who are essentially talking different languages without benefit of an interpreter—if they are to refrain from pounding their shoes on the table or on each other's heads. Lacking this charity, each will assume in the other a stubborn, if not perverse, obtuseness to hard-won values. As a consequence the painful history of religion is full of bitter disputations, culminating in burning stakes and pools of blood. We will indeed all be one, some day, when all manner of things are well, but this day waits until we all "grow up into him in all things, which is the head, even Christ" (Eph. 4:15).

Another "good" division comes inevitably to the advancing soul as mortification does its appointed work of bringing detachment. More and more as the years go by the spiritual person finds himself at odds with his surrounding world, which of course remains at a constant and fairly low level. In a non-snobbish sense he necessarily "outgrows the human race." He is divided against the world because of Christ—not angrily, not with hostility or hatred, but nevertheless with a weariness in his compassion. He is becoming less and less interested in it, less and less absorbed in it. Its pleasures, which years ago provided considerable joy, now offer almost no attraction at all.

This seems plain and clear enough as it is stated. In living fact it worries the most sincere people. To return to our opening thoughts, they feel that they should be in constant contact with other people in the great interests of unity and harmony. Since they know well that they must "love others as themselves" it seems to be treason, selfishness, and escapism that increasingly they desire solitude, quiet, the inner life. They have heard, and truly, that it is not good for man to be alone. They know, more clearly than any scoffer, that there is dynamic in the spiritual world which can unhinge human reason. They are apt to suspect, quite seriously, that they are going crazy. In their humility and in their zeal to

remain loyal to Christ's outgoing gospel, they are inclined
to fight hard against what is essentially his gentle disentan-
gling from a passing world.

This is not the place for discussion of valid worries along
those lines. In our outlined purpose we must stress the fact
that an invariable result of genuine spiritual development is
that we become more and more otherworldly as the years
go by. It is an invariable mark of advancing spirituality to
crave and to seek quiet and aloneness. It is an infallible sign
of growth to find one's surroundings, one's necessities, one's
wants, becoming ever more and more simple. One is, after
all, dwelling almost completely in the other world, not in
this one. In that world, increasingly, "but one thing is need-
ful; and Mary hath chosen that good part, which shall not
be taken away from her" (Luke 9:42).

As regards people, it is quite possible to love them more
and at the same time to like them less—certainly to need
them less. (There is ample evidence, not confined to that
scathing twenty-third chapter of St Matthew's Gospel, that
this was the case with our Lord.) Liking is emotional. It has
to do with personal attractions and natural feelings. Loving
has to do with the purified will; with our attitudes and actions
controlled by our purposed intentions. Thus we can love
our enemies—the phrase acknowledges that enemies do exist. We can work, pray, act, sacrifice, and otherwise spend
ourselves for the best interests of the person loved—whom
we may not like at all, and who certainly doesn't like us.

"Liking" is, in short, neither a very strong nor a very
strengthening thing. It is as weak as the way we feel at the
moment and it seldom rises higher than deeds. Loving is a
wholly different matter. It considers long-run results, which
it carefully carries out by plan and firm will. In addition it
relies a great deal upon the power of prayer to abet and to
overrule the power of works.

The increasing, but increasingly simple, prayer life of the developing spirit goes far toward solving, as well as creating, another poignant "division because of him." This is the matter of loneliness. Naturally the severances we have mentioned, and the ones we have not, leave one increasingly alone. And man is a lonely creature at best. The history of the world can most tellingly be read as the story of man's efforts to escape his loneliness, even as the history of religion is essentially the story of what God does about man's aloneness. Yet the very words that were spontaneously used in that last sentence—"loneliness" when speaking of natural man, "aloneness" when referring to religious man—indicate the essential difference. Without any rationalization at all, the communion of like minds concerned with the highest topics, the communion of saints, and communion with God are infinitely to be preferred to clubs, games, picnics, and parties as an antidote to, or a fulfillment of, the mere I. Indeed, a cocktail party has meaning at all only insofar as it foreshadows and in some degree partakes of the nature of Holy Communion.

This same immersion in the depths of prayer bears heavily on the last "division" to be mentioned here—that internal rending called "the broken heart" which is the especial lot of all sensitive people. Any such person does not live long in this world before he has his heart broken. Then, as life goes on, the broken heart will be further sundered into smaller and ever smaller pieces. This is especially the case, of course, with those who deliberately seek union with him whose heart the world insisted upon breaking one more time even after he died.

While the human heart is admittedly broken at any level and because of innumerable causes, rarefied souls undergo some especially shattering blows simply because they refuse adjustment to "reality with the top off." They desperately want to fly, yet they keep thudding back to earth. Their compassions widen while their resources shrink. Exposed on all fronts to the tragedy of earth they are ever sharpening their knowledge that the world is a lump of misery. They know to their vast sorrow what lies behind the happy smiling masks of their associates, those brave people. These and many other similar things they know—including the fact that they have deliberately asked for that poignant knowledge.

However, they also come to know that, without any question, the important thing is to let the world break the human heart. For one thing, there is room in the broken heart—and only there—for all the sorrows of the world. The broken heart—and only it—is curative, redemptive, of the wasteland around. In addition, it is the very raw material necessary for a strange and important alchemy which has been described in the words "Your sorrow shall be turned into joy" (John 16:20).

"Turned into joy" does not in the least degree connote "replaced by joy." The only really sufficient meanings of the former phrase, which the Church so rightly uses in the resurrection season, are found when one meditates upon it in connection with "Blessed are they that mourn, for they shall be comforted" (Matt. 5:4).

6 Decisions

Between our jumping out of bed in the morning and our falling back into it at night there are, especially in a high-pressure culture, literally hundreds of additional decisions we must make. The responsibility is always demanding, sometimes agonizing. To save wear and tear on his brain and his heart, the wise man reduces this daily burden by allocating as many decisions as possible to the department of habit. Far from holding any prejudice against sound habit, he makes one decision—to render habitual as much of the daily round as he can—thus sparing himself scores of other decisions each day. In so conforming to "heaven's first law," the principle of order, he has his desk cleared for whatever major action may arise.

He further dismisses, although not quite as summarily, dozens of other daily choices. If these are not items (such as whether or not he will brush his teeth) that can be solved in advance, still in a sense he has already made his decision about them. Far from holding any prejudice against sound authority, he refers many daily details to the proper expert. He telephones his printer or his lawyer; he calls in his engineer or his cost accountant; he consults his doctor or his priest—in order to act upon the sound guidance that specialized training has provided. He is not so pompous as to think that he himself knows everything, or that he is superior to the wisdom of the centuries codified in law—the civil law, the laws of health, the other laws of nature, the moral law.

This procedure leads most of us safely through most of our days, which are as routine as the methods of decision we have been outlining. However, into every life, no matter how thoroughly protected, there come occasions when we arrive at a fork in the road and are face to face with the vital distinction between an opportunity and a temptation. "The offer of this new work, with its greater responsibility and scope (not to mention salary and prestige)—should I accept it because it will crown my career, make complete use of my abilities, and really fulfill me? Or (there have been medical warnings) is this the time in my life—and my family's—when I should really begin to simplify my external relations rather than complicate them further?" The perceptive person frequently finds himself at such an unmarked crossroad, groping in the dark with a subtle decision that searches the central integrity of his being. He is well aware that the consequences of his choice will spread far beyond himself to involve the security, purpose, and meaning of life to a host of others. The spiritual man faces these delicate matters on the highest level of all. Decisions are not easier, but harder, for him because he has chosen to live in the borderland between law and Spirit.

Together with all other wise mortals he knows that the soundest possible choices must be made because, to view the matter only from the human side, we are free beings on a journey, and in order to arrive at journey's end we must take the correct turnings. Luck admittedly enters this picture, but life cannot be turned supinely over to luck. Intelligent effort is required.

Together with all other maturing people, he is increasingly becoming aware that his essential satisfactions proceed, not from his life's being what the surface minded call "happy" or "sad," a material success or failure, exciting or drab, gay or tragic, but whether or not his life is constructed on the lines of a sound story. It must have a pattern: a beginning, a middle, and an end. It must, in short, have meaning—a too rare overtone only produced when, as it were, the fingers of free will move across the strings of destiny.

Together with all other "moral" people he is profoundly aware that the most skillful rationalization will not permit his escape from ultimate accountability. He knows that each individual human life is a continuum under the constant scrutiny of the enormous fact of judgment, whether that subject be viewed theologically or merely psychologically. Psychology knows well that the "subconscious mind" takes its vengeance or bestows its reward both from moment to moment and at the end. Theology states this same truth in terms of "the soul" being under judgment both in the daily process and at the last great day. From either viewpoint "Heaven" and "Hell" are both rightly seen to be self-appointed ultimate destinies and inescapable present states. "All the road to Heaven is Heaven, and all the way to 'Hell' is Hell." We can *tell* which road we are on and, if we wish, continue on that road—the right one or the wrong one.

Beyond even this, the truly spiritual man sees decisions under the aspect of the eternal. Supremely aware that God is building a temple with the help of the material that we put into his hands, he recoils from forcing God to use scraps, like twisted motives and second-rate actions, in this building program. Even though he knows that God is perfectly capable of overruling inferior and evil decisions, still he wants to "free

God's energy" to forge ahead as fast as possible with his work. He wants to offer God the cleanest, straightest, most perfect lumber possible. In short, the spiritual man realizes that correct decision is not merely essential for his own sake, but for the sake of the whole universe which is in such terrible tension between good and evil. This principle, clearly discerned by everybody when, say, the decision is made to drop a hydrogen bomb, holds true even when we debate such a triviality as a cup of cold water. It is partly for practical reasons like this that the supreme activity of the human being is to know and love God increasingly, and thus increasingly to be in union with him and his purposes.

We have seen that in making our multidimensional decisions the intelligent beginning is made by consulting the law on the matter at hand. After this it is often useful to discuss the situation in all its ramifications with a carefully chosen person, in order to make as much use of "two heads are better than one" as that partial truth permits. This is not so much to seek advice, for the burden of our decision cannot be imposed upon another person. The purpose of discussion is largely to state the problem, and in that articulation possibly to discern it clearly for the first time. In thus crystallizing the issue we see the opposed columns of pros and cons, we view the situation as wholly as we can, we preview some of the probable consequences, we gain objectivity.

After these preliminaries we step over into the realm of the Spirit. Here we begin to use God's higher methods in order to gain God's surer results. To say this is not to cast aspersions on reason and intelligence, or to imply that they are not among God's methods. To decry human reason is blasphemy against the Giver of the precious gift; to arrive, by the use of human reason, at the conclusion that humans are irrational is ridiculous. The point is that intellectuality is only one way, and not the highest way, of knowing.

Faith, of course, is always the beginning step in any genuine knowledge of those elements that are in any sense "alive"—that are above the order of, say, sheer mathematics. In matters that matter *credo ut intelligam,* as St Anselm taught us long ago in his *Proslogion,* and as we incline to forget. "For I do not seek to understand in order that I may believe, but I believe in order that I may understand. For this also I believe—that unless I believed, I should not understand." Faith, far from being a perverse insistence upon "believing six impossible things before breakfast" each day, is a virtue which unites us with Truth.

Love is an even more penetrating way of knowing. Indeed, perfected love is the supreme unitive virtue; this level of love, far from being blind, constitutes sight. Only people who are full of love can possibly make right decisions, godlike decisions. We all acknowledge this by becoming sick at heart when, say, politicians in the thick of campaign battles reveal their vicious hatred before the unblinking eye of the television. We know in our bones that we are in for some bad decisions, and consequent trouble. However, it must suffice here to state rather dogmatically a truth which Father Harton substantiates at length: Human intelligence develops its highest powers and uses them rightly when strengthened by love and when protected by prayer.

For this reason we each make our own heart-decisions, which require certainty beyond that possible to the intelligence alone, in an atmosphere of steady, long-continued prayer. In this calm, protracted colloquy we are not simply talking with other humans, wise or unwise, but with Wisdom and Truth himself. Furthermore, in such an exercise he is talking with us—a fact which removes this practice from any reasonable charge of magic.

There is ample sober testimony that this approach brings about correct choices. The most subtle decisions, affecting whole lives and generations, can and do resolve into certainties when we give God time enough to make his loving will clear to our hard heads and hearts. A more important result of this practice is the clarification of motive. The end of the time available to us—a week, it may be—before we must decide can leave us in a condition like this: "I do not know, even yet. God has not shown me which course to take, or in my deafness I have not heard him. It may be that both courses are good and that one is merely higher. I do know now, however, that if I choose course X the motives will be entirely at my present level of development. Therefore I can take that course without a bit of fear or worry."

This is a sound conclusion because God uses motives, like love, to far better advantage than he uses wisdom. A decision based on honest motives works out so surely for good that it is entirely true to say that even if it is the wrong decision, it will be the right one.

It will be the right one on both of the important levels. The lower of these, we remember, is that of the maintenance of personal integrity. A man can everlastingly hold up his head (his moral head, if not his intellectual one) if he made his choice for pure and purified motives. He has followed his conscience which, while it is never infallible at any given moment, nevertheless must always be obeyed (even as it must always be educated).

On the higher level, of desire that the will of God be done, even if the decision is a mistaken one it works out well, because the living God can readily overrule when he has good honest motives to work with.

These observations lead naturally into the consideration of a morbid topic, scrupulosity, which is intimately although not solely connected with decisions. Scrupulosity lies in wait just off the beaten track, all coiled and ready to strike at any opportunity. It lies waiting especially for the most sincere and the most earnest. These are, of all people, the ones who are most aware of the impossibly high standards of the spiritual life and consequently most aware of the importance of decisions. If they make a fatal mistake which we shall discuss more thoroughly at the end of this chapter, they become morbidly rather than humbly aware of their own failure to live up to these high standards. In this condition they are especially prone to become obsessed with doubt, worry, and bad conscience. Thus inwardly tormented, they become outwardly impotent. "Fear hath torment" (1 John 4:18), and guilty fear the scrupulous have—rather, it has them, to the point where they can become totally ineffective.

It would be a sad thing if genuine Christianity could be rightfully accused of producing this morbid obsession in the human race—indeed this would be reason enough to abandon Christianity; but in spite of frequent charges this is simply not the case. Christianity, whose purpose is to lead us out of the house of bondage, has always been a joyous religion. It will never canonize a gloomy saint because it knows that gloom and sanctity are contradictory terms.

However, just as the Devil snaked his way into the original Garden of Eden, even so has he insinuated himself into that modern garden which is the Church. He has done his best, with considerable success in many areas of faith and practice, to corrupt Christianity as proclaimed from the pulpit and understood by the faithful. High on the list of his successes is this matter of scrupulosity. Some idea of the measure of this success can be gained from the sober assurances, coming from those who are in a position to know, that at least 75 per cent of the human race plods along under a heavy burden of guilt.

Of course a good deal of this is absolutely our own fault,

stemming from our pursuit of other values than the true ones or from our vacillating back and forth between truth and falsehood. On the other hand and, beyond any question, a great deal of it takes its rise from a devilish twisting of the truth about penitence and from a continuous harping on what is claimed to be morality—all of this harping being done in a strident voice on the general theme "Thou shalt not." As a result of what are called "Hell-fire and Damnation Tent Meetings" the notion is widely abroad that God is essentially a vicious ogre straight out of some distorted pages of the Old Testament, carrying brimstone and malice as standard equipment.

As one consequence, and in the name of sanity, many fine people have turned away from all organized religion in disgust, hostility, or indifference. They have wanted the Church to be like its Lord, and they quite correctly have failed to see the resemblance. Even more people, lacking this sturdy courage, have had to settle for an obsessed existence of the most fearful kind.

Sound theology must come to our rescue here. The fact of the matter is that God is our loving Father, with whom we live quite happily here and hereafter.

Sound morals are part of the rescue, too. St Augustine's famous *"Dilige et quod vis fac,"* which can be loosely translated "Love, and then do what you will," is as good a summary of the rules of really Christian behavior as any human has devised.

Above all, sound ascetics are necessary. They proceed from the realization that we are merely children, not yet gifted with the wisdom or strength to discern or to perform many important things. As in any healthy father-child relationship, whenever the child uses his best knowledge and motives and does the things he can, asking his father's help in the things he cannot, those things too come to pass. In pragmatic, hence anxious, America this truth needs stress that can be given to it by turning it around: All results are in God's department. Certainly we should "expect great things from God and attempt great things for God," doubtless with more fervor in both departments than we presently exhibit, but it is only God who "gives the increase" or who does not give it. One of the most deplorable of all fallacious thoughts in this connection is the twisted idea that religion consists in doing great things for God. It is far closer to the truth that religion consists in letting God do such things, or such nothings, as he chooses to do through us.

"I won't do it at all if I can't do it perfectly!" is a fine-sounding phrase, but a paralyzing one. Under the conditions stated, nothing gets done. Chesterton is far wiser on this subject, as he is on most, when he points out that if a thing is worth doing it is worth doing badly, rather than not at all. Chesterton had the habit of looking above and beyond the human, to God who gathers up the fragments that remain.

This leads to the ascetic point. Since the basic difficulty with the scrupulous is their unfortunate obsession with themselves, the cure for scrupulosity is the same as it is for all other forms of pride, which is the cultivation of the habit of looking out and away from the mere self; the habit of looking at God in all his love and power.

"I believe in God" is the fundamental spiritual exercise for the scrupulous and for everybody who is ridden by the hag of guilt. They must meditate on the glory, the forgiveness, and the omnipotence of God. They must wrench their fascinated gaze away from themselves, away from self-improvement manuals, away from morbid introspection, even away from their sins. It is far more important that sins are forgiven than that they are committed.

In brief, the scrupulous must take firm hold of that funny little mixed-up thing that is himself, hold it out at arms' length one last time, laugh at it if possible, and then drop it. From then on he will find ample occupation in loving God and his other children.

7 Mystical Experience

The phenomenon loosely and variously called mystical experience, spiritual experience, religious experience, includes a vast range of personal illumination which runs from the heights of piercing vision down to a passing moment of alerted awareness. In fact, the central purpose of this book is to stress that it can run "lower" than that. Rightly understood, religious experience, which does include the enjoyment of transported ecstacy, also involves resisting temptation, fighting doubt, paying one's taxes, performing distasteful jobs, taking the day's bitter along with its better, holding one's tongue on the proper occasions, suffering fools gladly, and an infinite variety of similar things. Religious experience, which is the totality of action and reaction with the totality of life, is nonetheless religious experience when it is unconnected with sacerdotalism and when it is not emotionally enjoyed or even emotionally experienced. The extraordinary, the occasional, the extrasensory, are not in the slightest degree the essential data of mature personal religion. No form of receiving is; there is something far more blessed than that. When with dedicated perseverance we are giving of ourselves, to God and to others, we are on the main track. There is considerable danger in the fact that spectacular matters like visions, transports, and voices always receive undue attention because of their very nature. Yet it is for this very reason that—especially in America, where religion has its history of "The Great Awakening," its disproportionate emphasis on the "Revival," its unwarranted stressing of emotional conversion—the subject demands brief surface consideration in a book of this kind.

Genuine intrusions from the other world into this one do occur; the evidence on the subject is simply too vast to be dismissed. (It should not be surprising that they do. God is, after all, quite real. Furthermore God is personal, we are persons, religion is a personal union between us, and personal relationships do have occasional flashes of intensity.) Because they do occur they provide us with important, if not basic, subject matter in the field of religion. Everybody with a mystical turn of mind should study the evidence in some standard work, such as Evelyn Underhill's *Mysticism*. Knowledge of the subject is singularly useful, for apologetic reasons, in our positivistic age. In addition, the personal religion of the mature Christian cannot but profit from a growing familiarity with the writings of the great seers. It is a most encouraging sign that students and publishers are making available in our day more and more of the classic material in this field. Equally encouraging is the fact that these publications find a large and responsive audience.

The manifold reports of tingling spiritual adventure indicate that mystical experiences take the greatest variety of forms. They can be flashingly momentary, or of brief measurable duration, or of considerable length in elapsed time. They can be visual, auditory, intellectual, or present themselves as an ineffable awareness which can be described as "super"-sensory or "non"-sensory. They can be of the sort wherein one simply looks through and perceives; when the mind stands still and only later races on to think out what it has glimpsed. On the other hand they can be, during the experience itself, a colloquy between the soul and God. They can take the form of visions of Christ, of what seems to be the Godhead itself, or of lesser spiritual beings like saints and angels. The Blessed Virgin Mary has, of course, been "seen" often.

It is necessary to add that the demons have been seen too, usually disguised as angels of light. This brings up an immediate and strong warning. Spiritualism, that conscious striving for messages from the dead, is consistently and rightly condemned by the Church on every count. The Church does not condemn spiritualism because it thinks that this dabbling with the occult is always pure fakery. Charlatans are not nice people, it is true, but they evoke more contempt than horror. The Church is primarily concerned because spiritualism has a dreadful, proven, ability to destroy souls. Its real danger is that it may actually put us in touch with the other world, on a diabolic level that is destructive in the extreme. The writer once knew, quite helplessly, a lady who was totally immersed in this practice, despite our Lord's clear warnings and direct commands on the subject. Her feet were entirely off the good solid ground of earth. She was not living her life today, in the here and now, which is the only possible time and place for the service of God. She offered a perfect illustration of the Devil's classic methods in that she was engaged in what might be, tomorrow or next year, in the never-never land. The whole ghastly episode was not so much dismal as frightening. It is horrible to see damnation looking out of the eyes of a living human.

We have, thus far, indicated that while spiritual "possession" can originate in God it can also take its rise in the lower world. Familiar experience testifies that the phenomenon can also occur, from entirely natural causes, in hysterical people. Hence our first reaction to such an experience should be to scrutinize it closely. In a sense the odds are two to one that it is not from God.

This scrutiny can be conducted through a simple test: If the revelation fits in with the historic faith, brings deeper personal certitude on matters of the faith already known, and consequently produces an energized inner peace, it is to be trusted. If, on the other hand, it is alarming, disturbing, and contrary to the faith it is certainly false—of the lower regions or of oneself. For example, a man of my acquaintance was once permitted to "see" the angels and archangels flooding the great sanctuary of Grace Church in Newark, New Jersey, during the singing of the Sanctus in the Holy Eucharist. He thoroughly appreciated the experience, to say the least, yet he recognized that essentially it only made more livingly real what he already knew intellectually. He made nothing of it, except a more fervent act of thanksgiving. The vision was undoubtedly genuine.

An important realization in this connection is that these extraordinary experiences are not to be sought after, stirred up, or in any way "worked for." Genuine ones are not in the realm of "our work" at all; they are objective and God sent, not subjective and self-caused. Should a person desire them to the point of deliberately striving after them he lays himself open to the greatest spiritual suspicion. He is manifestly desiring God's gifts, God's comforts, rather than desiring God. He is seeking excitement rather than the basic spiritual virtue of stability. If he really wants to undertake spiritual work of a constructive nature he should devote himself to achieving stability and perseverance, those greatest gifts that we can offer to God. Such occupation will keep him sufficiently employed.

We have already alluded to another connected point, which is that these experiences, even when they come spontaneously and are presumably genuine, should not receive disproportionate attention. The fact is that, for some reason, one is simply seeing more clearly what is always there. The spiritual atmosphere has thinned for a moment. For a while one sees through, discerning something of the shape of the mountain behind the mist. This is no credit to oneself, nor does the fact alter anything. The mountain was there all the time.

To take an extreme example of this: If after a vision one should decide to start a new religion which stemmed from the experience, he would be making a dire mistake. The fact that this mistake has often been made throughout human history does not affect the statement that it is only made by the uninstructed, the deluded, the untried, or the amateur of self.

Once again, this important subject is not central in the religious life. About all that a favored recipient of this special grace should do, after thanking God for his mercy in pulling the veil aside, is to pursue his regular business more zealously. In silence. There is no virtue in talking about these matters, except when occasion and charity really demand it. What an anomaly it would be if having a vision or two should make one conceited, instead of having the effect produced in St Thomas Aquinas. His final vision, in which he knew things that simply cannot be uttered, led him to lay his mighty pen aside forever.

For all that, there are undoubted benefits which derive from these experiences. One great corporate benefit is that they help make manifest to a dull world the reality of the spiritual realm, which so often is vague and elusive to the point of being non-compelling for many. Lourdes is surely a good thing for the world, especially in our secular era.

On the personal level, we are stimulated to renewed effort when we study the insights gained by the great ones in their mystic experiences. St Paul, St Teresa, St John of the Cross, Juliana of Norwich, and countless others have set down in halting words something of the reality of their inner life with God. As we grope to understand the truth which their words try to express, the things that they have seen and known come somewhat home to us. Their experience lifts, ennobles, and reassures us. This may well be another of the reasons why God lets these things happen.

Finally, if one should himself be granted a genuine experience of this kind he will be even more firmly strengthened in his faith. In a most special way he will have "tasted and seen how gracious the Lord is" (Ps. 34:8). Long years of normal religious life have prepared the way for this moment, by leading to considerable knowledge of God—who is indeed knowable, if not perfectly so. As a culmination of this continued interplay between Person and person there comes the intrusion through which God makes himself unmistakably known. From that point on the soul has something that can hardly be taken from it. Technically considered, it has developed "wisdom," that gift of the Spirit which enables us to have experience of God, to the point where it can cry out "I know!" Henceforward, even during the nights that will surely come in the future, it has something behind itself that it can draw on. During the coming days that momentary call, "Friend, come up higher and taste of me" (cf. Luke 14:10), will be the strongest possible incentive toward definite spiritual progress.

8 Acedia

"Heaviness, gloom, coldness, sullenness, distaste and desultory sloth in work and prayer, joylessness and thanklessness . . . do we not know something of the threatenings, at least, of a mood in which these meet? The mood of days on which it seems as though we cannot genuinely laugh, as though we cannot get rid of a dull or acrid tone in our voice; when things . . . look as dismal as a flat country in the drizzling mist of an east wind; days when we might be cynical if we had a little more energy in us; when all enthusiasm flags out of our work; when the schemes which we have begun look stale and poor and unattractive as the scenery of an empty stage by daylight; days when there is nothing that we *like* to do."

Thus writes Bishop Paget, in *The Sorrow of the World*, as he describes the beginning symptoms of *acedia*. The word, variously spelled *accidie,* is found nowadays only in the larger dictionaries. It is an old word for an old, old sin which is widespread in our modern world. The chances are excellent that every reader of this book either has been, is, or will be afflicted by its spiritless torpor, especially in his middle years when life has been daily for a long time and promises to be exceedingly daily for a long time into the future. The depressing subject must be thoroughly understood, first by way of a more complete description.

A person in the grip of acedia has drifted so far out of the current of things that from where he lies motionless by the shore he hardly bothers to watch life go by. He is sullenly bored with himself, with his job, with the whole world, and with God. There is no worthwhileness anywhere. Nothing gives any pleasure or promises any. He wants nothing, in every sense of that phrase except the good one. In desolate dejection of spirit he simply goes "out and hides his Lord's money," except that he does not go far nor dig a deep hole. His talent merely drops to the earth beside him and lies there. Along with everything else, it isn't worth bothering about. The victim, lacking interest in everything, exists in a "listless, joyless, fruitless, hopeless, restless indolence, more tiring and exacting than the hardest work, more sensitive in its dull fretfulness than any state of bodily suffering," as Paget so well puts it.

In the *Inferno* Dante is writing of acedia when he reports the lament eternally issuing from beneath the swamp in the Fifth Circle: "Gloomy were we in the sweet air that is gladdened by the sun, carrying sullen, lazy smoke within our hearts; now lie we gloomy here in the black mire." The passage hints that acedia lies close to the sin against the Holy Ghost, the sin against life itself, in being so directly opposed to the fruits of the Spirit which include "love, joy, peace" (Gal. 5:22). Dante is right. Lack of enthusiasm means, if words mean anything, that we are not in God nor he in us.

Chaucer, in *The Pardoner's Tale,* especially singles out peevishness, irritation, and ill temper as characterizing acedia, and begins to cope with its causes when he writes that "bitterness is mother of accidie." St Thomas Aquinas notes this same close causal connection between acedia and

envy. Any full analysis of the springs of acedia would, however, be as subtle and complex as the sin itself. Sheerly physical items, like the physical and emotional exhaustion which
are so prevalent in our rapid-fire society, are often heavily
involved. The climate of general opinion plays a strong part.
It is remarkable that Paget could write, in 1890: "If a considerable number of articles in magazines imply that it is
impossible to know God, it does not seem worth while to
get up half an hour earlier in the morning to seek Him before the long day's work begins; if, in various quarters and on
various grounds, the claims of Christ are being set aside or
disregarded, then, though the arguments against those claims
may never have been carefully examined, the standard of the
Sermon on the Mount begins to seem more than can be expected of a man; and if it is often hinted that sins which
Christianity absolutely and unhesitatingly condemns may
be condoned in an ethical system which takes man as it finds
him, and recognizes all the facts of human nature, the reso-
lute intention of the will is shaken, and the clear, cherished
purpose of a pure and noble life recedes further and further,
till it almost seems beyond the possibility of attainment, beyond the range of reasonable ambition."

The pressure of society upon our souls today is not so new
then, after all. We may have new phrases, like "adjustment
to the attainable," to describe the condoning of mediocrity,
the watering down of any real sense of duty, sacrifice, and
worth which can produce acedia in a whole civilization. We
may have new words, like "meaninglessness" and "futility,"
to substitute for "acedia" itself. The essential facts remain
the same, however, as when Paget so penetratingly discerned
them more than seventy years ago.

For the special purposes of this book we can be led back by
Paget himself to the early part of the fifth century, when
Cassian correctly proclaimed the fact that acedia is supremely

likely to afflict the religious. Henry Sidgwick, in his *Outline of the History of Ethics,* may be following Cassian when he writes: "In particular the state of moral lassitude and collapse, of discontent with self and the world, which is denoted by 'Acedia', is easily recognizable as a spiritual disease peculiarly incident to the cloister." Those last five words hint at the truth, discerned by all students of the inner life, that the most advanced form of acedia is found especially among those who cultivate the spiritual life deeply.

Some of the reasons for this are readily apparent. Our physical nature, in its fallen state, is ill-adapted to the strains that Spirit puts upon it; exhaustion, with its consequences, is an always lurking danger for poets and prophets alike. A connected fact is that the contemplative life is one sided at best, and perilously so if one forgets that *laborare est orare.* To take St Benedict's wisdom on its very lowest plane, the big muscles of the body will have either their exercise or their revenge.

The intangible nature of the spiritual life, both in regard to personal progress and to external achievement, is also in point. Only rarely does one really *know* that the perfect offering of the liturgy is indeed man's supreme work; many years can go by before this satisfying knowledge pays a second visit. In the interval a contractor, say, can often have savored the many concrete satisfactions involved in building six new factories and making a million dollars. Furthermore, an unhealthy perversion of right-proportioned introspection threatens the spiritually minded, tempting them to watch their own sensations overmuch—a paralyzing occupation. Life is much easier for those who handle brick and mortar than for those who wield a pen. It is hardest of all for those who hold nothing whatever in their hands.

Even if these pitfalls are not fallen into, there is another trap just beyond. Like all people with deep knowledge of life, the spiritually mature know its razor-edge character sometimes too well for their own good. While fools rush in to many situations where the more perceptive rightly fear to tread, on the other hand this very awareness can keep them from adventures which they really ought to take. Their aloneness is an added difficulty here. Too seldom is anyone else in view to spur them on by word or example. The temptation is strong to rest in a position safely attained—a spiritual impossibility, for to do this is to bank the fires of love. Acedia is the inevitable result.

Finally, in these hints as to why those who are well advanced in the spiritual life are prime targets for the "sickness that destroyeth at noonday" (Ps. 91:6), we must remember that the Devil fears their activity and their example above that of all others. If he can produce in them a paralysis of effort toward the highest good he kills two birds with one stone. He bags big game, and by the capture of this leadership ensures that the rank and file will fall more easily into line.

The gloomy "sickness unto death" that is acedia is among the most difficult things in the world to combat, because it contains within itself the all-but-perfect resistance to the only means of its own cure. The malady encloses its victim in a circular cage, for there isn't enough life left to want any more life. Since there is no desire, nothing is desirable; there is no response to invitation because nothing invites. "Standing there all the day idle" (cf. Matt. 20:6) in boredom actually leads to more boredom and increased lethargy, which produce a group of petty vices tending to increase the original discontent. Spouses and friends find themselves in a most baffling, and unenviable, predicament.

The victim of acedia must, of his own initiative, do an almost impossible thing. He must seize himself firmly and hurl himself back into life. He must begin a process—almost any process will do; the essential point is to get started at something—that breaks through that circular situation in which he is trapped.

This is accomplished, as all worth-while things are, by thought, prayer, and work. These are always the elements which bring happiness and growth here and hereafter; it is axiomatic that the times we feel least inclined toward them are the times when they must be most strenuously employed. (Incidentally, a person should go off on a Retreat exactly at the time when he is too busy to consider such a thing. Activisim is not being proclaimed here in general, only in this particular.) Their application is particularly apt in the case of acedia, whose own voice St John Climacus lets us hear, saying "My adversaries are the singing of psalms and the labour of the hands; the thought of death is my enemy, but that which kills me outright is prayer, with the sure hope of glory."

The supine soul must make himself meditate upon God's mighty acts in creation, redemption, and sanctification. He must forcibly think back to the times, the occasions, and the places when he himself found life good. These nauseating thoughts he should hold firmly before himself. By a similar process he should force himself to realize that others have attacked life with rewarded enthusiasm. He must convince himself that right here, in this horrible town among these grotesque people, others have zest, others grow from life to life and from the exercise of talent to more talent.

Then he must be up and doing—it is impossible to be specific in this regard; we repeat that it can be almost anything large or small—by dint of sheer will power. This breakthrough may well have to be continued by effort applied daily for months, until life begins to flow back through the channels thus created. One can be certain that daily rationaliza-

tion will present almost irresistible appeals against one's
spiritless efforts.

Prayer, which is the third thing that the dying spirit must
engage in, will require at least as much effort as his thought
and his work. Prayer is the last thing that the victim of acedia
is interested in. He has no taste for God at all, so if he thinks
about him it will only be in sullen terms like "Lord, I know
thee that thou art a hard man, reaping where thou dost not
sow" (Matt. 25:24). This grumble of the man who hid his
talent is true enough, in the sense that it expresses what the
man really believed. The fact that he had the matter totally
wrong only underlines the point that in the deep depression
of acedia we must force ourselves to meditate on the truths
of revelation which tell what God is really like.

A final bitter thought is that the victim must go to church
and use the sacraments. He will revolt against the effort
involved. He will recoil at the thought of the dreary people
who will of necessity be there, each sporting a dismally smiling face and calling cheerful greetings across the square.
Above all he will have no taste whatever for penance, communion, or worship, those only means whereby God can
come into him and lift him out of himself.

Yet this threefold way is the only method through which
his dying embers can be rekindled. Only by seeing life and
God as they are, by praying to God to stir up his will, and
then by forcing himself to put the prayer into action, will our
sodden soul become once more a human being—a rational
animal with God in his heart, walking through life purpose-
fully with his feet on the ground and his head in the air.

9 Come Up Higher

The proverb "You can lead a horse to water but you can't make him drink" hints strongly at a particularly poignant aspect of God's dealings with us—his problem of inducing us to accept what he freely offers. Our own experience has brought us sharp knowledge of the potential heartbreak involved in the inviolable gift of free will. What teacher has not known bitter disappointment at his failures to impart knowledge and vision? What poet has not despaired of conveying his dreams? What artist has not wept when beauty stood unseen before blind eyes?

Even leaving unmentioned the frustrations connected with sheer communication between people, there remains the fact that in personal relationships the receiver is quite as important as the would-be giver. Creative interplay demands a responsible receiving apparatus which cannot come into existence without desire. How does one unblock this secret spring of motivation? Not by exasperation's method of knocking its victim unconscious or using lesser force that pushes him around—"playing God" is a far more subtle matter than what the man in the street means by the phrase. God will indeed use enormous pressure to gain our ends, but he will not prick our soap bubble with his irresistibility. He respects that greatest human glory which is our ability to miss, or to attain, a genuine Heaven. He knows supremely well that if we are to enter into this reality we have to hurl experiments against its wall, catch them on the rebound, evaluate the results, and then try the whole thing over again from different angles.

These truths lie behind the unalterable fact that when God is preparing to do something great for us, he always asks something first. When, for example, the time comes for us to enjoy the spine-tingling view from the top of the next hill, God's essential problem is to induce us to take the first step. The remainder of the journey requires far less energy than breaking through the original inertia.

The negative side of this fact was the theme of the last chapter. We turn now to consider the positive side—that when we say "yes" to a prompting of God we open a switch that lets his current flow through. This is why "Whatsoever he saith unto you, do it" is the most important advice in the world. It is the way that miracles happen, everywhere we look.

To take an illustration from the intellectual realm: We feel a stirring of curiosity about a problem. When we respond with study, research, application, trial and more trial, the results can be overwhelming. The astonishing story of science in the last century teems with examples of the fundamental truth that we do not steal knowledge from a grudging God. He gladly gives what we make ourselves ready to appropriate.

Psychology can supply endless illustrations of how, often after long years of pressure, God finally prompts us to stagger a few halting steps out into the arena to face a dragon whose glance has always before turned us to stone. Sweating and shaking, in his power we lift up our heads and look our demon in the eye, whereupon it falls over dead. The spell is broken. We are reborn into a world of larger freedom.

In the spiritual realm the supreme illustration of our point is the annunciation story, where, with everything in the world hanging on a young girl's response, we may well imagine that the very archangels held their breath until Mary said, "Be it unto me according to thy word." Another familiar example chosen from the legions available in every authentic account of God's relations with man is the story of "the miraculous draught of fishes." At the conclusion of a sermon given from a fishing boat moored a little from the shore, Christ makes a suggestion to the owner of the craft: "Launch out into the deep and let down your nets for a draught" (Luke 5:4).

This particular story in illustration of the ways of God with man is an especially lovely thing to ponder if only because in its telling it uses so many haunting phrases. The most poignant of them gives this book its title. Another—"Launch out into the deep" along with me—bristles with suggestive implications, only one of which is that God takes the highest possible view of us. He does not consider it worthy of us to be paddling around "a little from the land." However, the fundamental reason this story is chosen from among the available hundreds is not the stylistic one, but rather that in its telling it moves quickly through the invariable spiritual progression.

First there is God's prevenience, or initiating suggestion—"launch out." In the next sentence we note the typical human hesitancy, founded upon experience of futility, to accept God's invitation. The owner of the fishing boat, Peter, said—for all of us, so many times—"we have toiled all the night and taken nothing," which constitutes that "what's the use?" which we discussed in the preceding chapter from one angle and which we shall examine from another point of view in the chapter after this. However, Peter went on to add the all-important affirmation, "Nevertheless, at thy word I will let down the net." The result was an astonishing catch of fish that filled Peter's boat and his partners' as well. This, however, is not the end. In a swift sentence or so the story moves to its proper climax, affording a classical expression of the truth we are exploring. This point is that, whereas Peter could see no further than catching fish when he said "yes" (and then did so in abundance) Christ was able to open his eyes to greater possibilities by saying, "From henceforth thou shalt catch men." God, who speaks in parables, always takes the limited literal handle we give him and then steps up the frequency. He leads not only Peter, whose whole apostolate depended upon his reluctant yes, but all of us into regions that we never dreamed existed.

It is time to go more slowly, now that we have sketched out this law of growth "in the round," for every reader can recall occasions in his own experience when it apparently stopped working. "Recall" is, in fact, too weak a word in this connection. Some of our most vivid, searching, and disquieting memories cluster around those many times when we toiled diligently all through the night of many years and still took nothing.

It needs to be said categorically, and realized categorically, that the law never does stop working. We are dealing here with a more fundamental part of the universe than the law of gravity, in the sense that it will not be repealed even should the conditions arise when gravity is. (Since we can in some sense imagine a state of affairs when "matter" does not exist, even if we have to go back before creation to accomplish this feat, we can in that sense imagine a state of affairs when the laws affecting matter are suspended. It is impossible, however, for a believer in the Eternal Trinity to conceive of a condition in which the laws of personal relationship would not operate.) Our searing memory of multitudes of unrewarded efforts must, then, force us to study the total situation most carefully.

This close scrutiny will show that a great many of the questions that seem to orbit this area are really planets of another system. In this book, for example, they are examined under other headings. Others, like subtle matters of human delusion, lie beyond our proposed scope. The remaining ones that are really germane to the present context lie in the realm of mistaken value judgments.

We have, in the first place, a strong tendency to romanticize. This very chapter has used the expression "Peter's apostolate," which is a fine form of words indeed. From our vantage point, which looks back on his heroic career, it is a valid form of words. The New Testament shows, however, that in the process of living out the daily grind of that "apostolate" Peter was blind, on occasion, to the romance of it all. The record states a host of frustrating disappointments, and hints at many more. The greatest of these, without doubt, came on that horrible Friday when everything he had bet his life on died before his very eyes. Here indeed was the night and the nothing, to the extent that everybody understands and can sympathize with his betrayal.

The point is that God did indeed do something very great in Peter, producing a rocklike character from a volatile, enthusiastic, up-and-down raw material. Peter's own humble and willing crucifixion at the end of many dusty years tells that story. However, even being crucified upside down is neither a romantic nor a rewarding experience on the surface, when we come to think of it. A severe alteration of values is required in order to see how it fulfills the promise that he would catch men.

Closely connected with this necessary shift of values is

another item involving our growth. Early in the spiritual life, often at the time of conversion, great and astonishing "catches of fish" usually occur. This is in the very nature of things. There is a violent and observable change in the character, say, of an alcoholic who finally "comes to himself"— a most comforting phrase from the parable of the prodigal son, implying as it does that the true self all along was not the prodigal one. The demon is cast out and the people marvel. After this, however, in response to our arrested alcoholic's further "yeses" to God, nothing so miraculous happens. The new man is merely able to work steadily and satisfactorily at his job. His home life straightens up, so that his children lose their terror and his wife her tears. Is the less dramatic less important? Are the long years of sober joy to be regarded as the failure of God?

In short, while the urgent cry to God to "do something great in me" is entirely valid and indeed God caused, in most situations its sheer necessity lessens as the process of sanctification goes on. The temple of one's body does not need to be so violently cleansed again, after the initial overthrowing. Increasingly after that one begins to see the hand of God in the "little" things. The many things he has yet to say to us are spoken in a quieter voice and said more slowly. The ways of God with men in the sanctifying years are the ways of a sower, and of seed that lies dormant until its time comes, and which even then develops to its maturity only by gradual stages. It is to misread truth to expect that, throughout these long slow decades, God will be seen on a chariot of fire in the clouds of heaven. It is sheer adolescent emotionalism to keep on desiring an unending succession of thrills. The mature soul, indeed, far from craving an experienced annual revival rightly learns to be suspicious of all such "signs and wonders." He has come to discern God in mangers, in poverty, in the still small voice, in a few drops of water, and in the breaking of a tiny piece of bread. Increasingly he knows, with increasing satisfaction, "How silently, how silently, The wondrous gift is given."

The radical difference between the growth processes characteristic of the two worlds, already noted in the chapter on humility, merits restating here in a different way—which expands a few trenchant sentences by Frank S. Cellier in his brilliant paper "The Liturgical Movement and the Ministry of the Laity" (*The Eucharist and Liturgical Renewal*). In so far as it is at all valid to analyze by separating into its component parts the usual story of success in this world, the familiar progression has a strong tendency to begin with enormous emphasis on "doing." This great and even sacrificial activity is aimed at "possessing" certain external items called "treasure on earth." Only after a man has reached the point when he must tear down his barns and build bigger ones in order to hold all this treasure is there much time for him to consider the matter of "being." The thought of this is characteristically deferred until the retirement years, when it is usually too late. The well-known emotional dangers of retirement help document the truth that a human being stunted by six decades of dealing only with the surface of things is too set in his ways to begin discovering, then, the meaning of all those facts.

Although one must be cautious here, for "doing" and "being" interact upon each other in a non-separable way, in the spiritual world this process is pretty much the reverse. Here the main emphasis is always on "being"; on developing his only real possession; on "becoming what he is." Involved in this, and after this, it might please God that there be some doing. Just as readily it might not, for "they also serve who only stand and wait." This whole truth applies supremely to possessing, when that word is limited to material possessions. These things are essentially so indifferent that they do not matter much one way or the other. God can be served in utter material simplicity, or in the far more difficult way that is the vocation of the steward of great riches. Since this is a matter of particular vocation, the choice rests entirely with God.

The final, definitive illustration of this whole subject of "values" is the crucifixion of Christ, which was the result of his final "yes" to his Father. Naturally this cannot be discussed here, or anywhere, in an exhaustive manner; the following approach may well not be the most fruitful one. However, the fact is that there was a steady development in our Lord's human understanding of things; we are told that he "increased in wisdom" over the years. Stages of this development can be discerned in the synoptic Gospels (not in St John) ranging from "I must be about my Father's business" (Luke 2:49), through the upsurge of knowledge about himself at his baptism, through his transfiguration experience, and finally at the Cross.

At this culminating moment he was, it would seem, caught in the dilemma of knowing he was the Messiah and yet that the Messiah must die—an unthinkable paradox to Jewish minds. How does a dead king bring in a kingdom? But our Lord's faith in the "yes" to the Father held firm, of course, so he went to his death in sure and certain hope of some sort of resurrection.

The multitude of fish that were enclosed by this net which was let down into the depths for a draught have not yet been counted.

10 Discouragement

A characteristic temptation of all maturity, and par excellence of the maturing spiritual life, is to discouragement.

The beginning reasons for this paradoxical situation, nowhere better stated than in the book of Ecclesiastes, inhere in the fact that over the dusty years we amass a great deal of sobering knowledge about human limitations in general and our own incapacities in particular. Youth, quite naturally, cannot possibly appreciate these strange fruits of experience. In that immortal phase of the mortal career the typical convictions are that life offers every possibility and that the world is our personal oyster. Youth's built-in optimism, accepting uncritically the philosophy of Horatio Alger, really expects to move from rags to riches within six diligent months, to marry the boss's daughter at the end of the year, and to live happily ever after. Maturity, on the other hand, knows very personally what a struggle it is merely to stay even with the opposed current, let alone advance against it. Maturity can amply testify to the fact that hopes fail, dreams vanish, the fondest aims continually elude. It knows a great deal about the shortness of human life, the smallness of its

94

stage, the limitations of its scope. Age can indeed join youth
in saying that "man's reach exceeds his grasp." It will, however, mean something quite different by the phrase.

This developing knowledge, so pregnant with discouragement, about our stubborn environment is most acute in the
maturing life of the spirit. In the beginning we gladly seized
a flaming torch because nothing mattered save concern that
the world be remade on the lines of its original purpose. The
task seemed relatively simple then. God himself was working
toward this end, and the dismal tyranny of the world's Dark
Ages was long since over. But now, with the increasing application of science to life, with the extension of education,
with the use of psychological insights, medical skill, and so-
ciological improvements to add to the power of earnest
prayer, his kingdom would shortly be manifest. In the result-
ing Shangri-La everyone would sit under his vine and under
his fig tree enjoying a relaxed millennium.

Alas for dreams. The years have brought home to us, as
they have to all previous generations, the unchanging fact
that the world does not take flame readily from the matches
we apply to it. Candid observation recognizes that this is
partly because the kindling is exceedingly damp. The same
frankness acknowledges that it is also true because we ourselves are not so hot. We remember, too well, our own history. With honest folk the remembrance of things past is
always the remembrance of compromise, frailty, and sloth re-
sulting in potentialities thrown away, opportunities neglected, and greatness forfeited.

The temptation to spiritual discouragement gains triple
strength from this universal experience—firstly because of
the deeper insights we gain about the nature of spiritual rewards. In the beginning we thought that as the spiritual life
progressed it would become easier in itself and in addition
would make all other things more simple. Our cleared eyes

now note that, while the promise of reward for spiritual effort is indeed quite structural to the Bible, one of the most typical statements of the character of this reward is "thou hast been faithful in a few things; I will make thee ruler over many things" (Matt. 25:21). Experience has taught us that this means what it says—more work with more responsibilities. We realize that with spiritual development, as with all maturity, the difficulties rather than the zest of life come to the fore. The rewards for work done are in the nature of heightened capacities for greater work remaining to be done. If this is because we are in many senses stronger, the fact remains that we are also considerably more tired.

Secondly, we have come to know the potentially discouraging nature of this our work—that it does not, cannot, advance the kingdom of God in any observable sense. When we were neophytes we were supremely encouraged by Jesus' claims, overshadowing all his other claims, that in him the kingdom of God was launched with new power. We noted with assurance how he cited his spiritual activities to substantiate this claim—"go and tell John the things you see and hear" (Luke 7:19); "if I with the finger of God cast out devils, no doubt the kingdom of God is come upon you" (Luke 11:20). However, over the years the contrast of this supreme assertion with the observable fact that the world is not much bettered since the Incarnation has caused us vast searching of our spiritual hearts on many levels, including that low ebb of doubt in which we wrestled with the fundamental question "Was Jesus wrong?" Only through agonized study and prayer did we come to know that Jesus was talking about God's kingdom, not ours; God's intrusion from above, not our building from below. In this realization we stayed faithful to the heavenly vision, content to let the seed grow secretly until the appointed time. Yet, even if we avoided all temptation to "transcendental irresponsibility" as we went about our

daily round, there was strong feeling of discouragement as
the ego plodded through what it considered a "martyrdom
of meaninglessness."

Thirdly, exactly because in the cultivation of spiritual
values we come to see more clearly the greater glory that is
potentially around and within, we realize that our whole
personal calling is to the impossible. Like mountain climbers,
we are seeing clearer and wider horizons as we ascend from
peak to higher peak. Unlike their physical panorama, however, the expanding spiritual vision has an effect that is apt
to paralyze further effort. St John grandly writes "When HE
shall appear we shall be like him!" (John 3:2). A lesser spirit
than St John, seeing with sufficient clarity what HE is like, is
prone to respond "Who—me? I, who am beginning to learn
something about myself, am going to be made into *that* sort
of person?" The situation becomes increasingly discouraging
with each advance, precisely because each new pinnacle dis-
closes a vaster range on a new horizon. One is strongly
tempted to settle for something more attainable. Entertainment of this thought opens the door to misery, for sloth is
only the first child of discouragement. Hard on its heels come
doubt, bitterness, cynicism, and ultimate despair, swiftly
followed by all the deadly offspring of that fertile daughter
of pride.

Fortunately, discouragement readily grinds away that
brashness which is the bane of the untried. It strongly urges
a healthy self-examination upon our complacency. Thus it
seeks its own antidote by leading us, as few other pressures
can, to prayer, to humility, to dependence upon the power
of God.

Theology, the science of sanity, has always known that
human encouragement derives from God. It consistently
proclaims divine power, not human impotence, because its

habit of looking at God brings conviction that the universe itself no more than hints at his available resources. In our day theology has a most interesting handmaiden which may well prove healthy for all of us. Prone to make God in our own image, we are easily discouraged because a God of that stature is far too small. Modern emphasis on astronomy can only be healthy for our theology if we use it to help make real what the seers, like Isaiah, have always known. It is no accident that all the world's great religions were born in the East, on the open deserts under the slowly turning stars.

Acquaintance with the universe around us, acquired either through books or a telescope, is an especially healthy spiritual pursuit for city man. The city-dweller's preoccupation with human affairs practically forces him to miss his eternal backdrop. He is under frantic pressure to live in a destructive hurry. Astronomy can give him renewed insight into God's power, the essential antidote to human discouragement, together with especial insight into the aspect of God's power which we call time. God has all those light years at his disposal for making something out of us; the fact that he uses them in dealing with a temporary affair like a material universe points to this realization beyond any question. After all, God values *value* far more than he does things, just as we do. It is from him, indeed, that we get our ideas on this subject.

By thus enlarging our vision, science can go far toward opening our ears to the merciful teaching consistently presented by orthodox Christianity that human perfection need not be attained during the few years of our earthly life. This is especially encouraging to a soul who is certain that in his own case it is highly unlikely that it will be. Astronomy could remind him, and millions of others, of the historic teaching about the interim state, variously called Paradise or Purgatory, which may well follow upon the earthly probation of the vast majority of human beings.

It is precisely the people with the deepest conception of human potential and of human limitation on earth to whom the simple eschatology of "either Heaven or Hell" immediately after earthly life is unreal and desolating. To them it makes a mockery both of human life and of God. They feel that if only those who reach perfection by the time of their death "go to Heaven" and the rest "to Hell," then the traffic after, say, that unhappy day at Hiroshima must have been quite one sided. To them the "either Heaven or Hell" alternative charges God with being nearly a total failure in bringing up his children. Under these conditions God would be a very unhappy parent, and a most unfair one in addition—for the majority of human beings, up to the present, came to their deaths before they had had much of an opportunity in the process sketched in this book. And of course there is no magic in the act of death, or at any other time. There are no irresistible sacraments, no hypodermic injections of Spirit, waiting to render inconsequential our cooperative efforts in the adventure of living.

Orthodox Christianity, like its Lord, knows this too and has always held open the merciful and realistic probability that at death we enter a state visited long ago by the penitent on the Cross. There, "in Paradise"—not waiting or sleeping or stagnating; yet without chance of failure, for life on earth will have fixed the direction—we keep on with the process of growth that began on earth. We expand with the expanding galaxies, which may be the parabolic reason why the galaxies seem to do just that.

Certainly the eternal reassurance to discouragement is rooted and grounded in the fact that Christ himself is the one who said, "Keep on asking, and without any question you will ultimately receive." This authoritative source is not "merely" God, but also God in our common life. Best of all, he did not throw the words out easily in the bright sunshine of a promising early ministry. He used another form of them at the dismal ending of the whole dwindling affair when he said "Father, into thy hands I commend my spirit" (Luke 23:46).

"Ask and ye shall receive" (John 16:24)? Once the fields were white to the harvest, but those adulating crowds drifted away as his message became more and more searching, to increase in numbers again only in the form of a howling mob. Even the few persevering disciples had, each in his own way, betrayed him, denied him, forsaken him. Still he proclaimed the Fatherhood of God and, unable because of nails and ropes to persevere in any other way, he kept on commending that essential element which impels all other "keepings on"—an unconquerable spirit. He was certain to the end that continuous seeking brings achievement even, indeed especially, when all the circumstances of achievement are entirely missing. All circumstances except *the* circumstance, which is God.

The questing spirit, expressed without let-up in our work and our prayer, is the high vibrant level of perseverance, that greatest quality which a human being can bring to life. Essentially all we have to do is keep on "asking and seeking and knocking," in terms of our present understanding. The result can only be one of two things: either an ultimate "yes" to our continuous assault, or an ultimate "no" that is assigned to divert the pressure of our search toward what God really has in mind. The pressure of this continuing stream overflows the dam of his living resistance, moving everything to a higher level. This is the level of his will, as contrasted to ours.

There are those who proclaim that with persistent application and intercession we can always get what we ask for.

On its low level this delusion proceeds from a simplified and distorted view of the nature of reality combined with an equation of religion with magic. This utterly violates Christ's teaching, from which proceeds our whole thesis that God loves us too much and values us too highly to give us what we want in place of what we need. Its high-level advocates— such as Aldous Huxley when he wrote *The Perennial Philosophy*—warn us against our petitions because the supernatural world is so constructed that we can indeed get what we ask for. There are at least two safeguards against this disaster. The more trustworthy of these is that same fundamental fact of God's Fatherhood, which will certainly not give us a scorpion in place of our requested fish, and in many cases will not give us the fish either. The second safeguard is our own cultivated humility, which after a hundred "noes" from God might begin to try to see why he is so obdurate.

St Paul, not universally conceded to be a humble man, nevertheless demonstrated this spirit after only three casts of his net instead of the average hundred. He constitutes a standing illustration in this field. "There was given me a thorn in the flesh," he tells us (2 Cor. 12:7). Some think it was epilepsy; certainly it was something not merely undesirable but apparently crippling to the work to which he was certain he had been called. "For this thing I besought the Lord thrice, that it might depart from me." The repeated petition was denied, and through the denial St Paul learned the deep wisdom that "My grace is sufficient for thee; for my strength is made perfect in weakness."

His experience is a perpetual warning against the too easy assumption that, in emphasizing "seek and ye shall find," God is promising to give us what we ask. This is not so at all, as one of the great dawning lights of maturity assures us. The promise means that we are going to find *something* if we

keep on seeking. In the power and love of God this something will be a far greater matter than the thing we were
looking for.

If they had not learned this from considerable experience,
the saints would have stopped interceding long ago. Always
to get what they wanted and in wanting asked for, would be
too dreadful and impoverishing a fate to contemplate. They
were steeped in that Psalm verse "And he gave them their
desire, and sent leanness withal into their soul" (Ps. 106:15)
which has so much to say to our secular world, but they kept
on with their pursuit because they knew their prayers were
censored and transmuted. They had learned to look for the
gold of his giving rather than the lead of their asking. The
essential point is that they kept on.

It has already been indicated several times that the greatest
"gold" is the increasing discovery that God is running our
lives; that we ourselves really are not. This awareness of
Divinity shaping our ends is, of course, one of the greatest
indications of growth in the understanding of life. It is also
the supreme antidote to discouragement. Discouragement
without hope it would certainly be if our careers were solely
in our own hands—if we actually were, by some ill chance,
the masters of our fates and the captains of our souls. Experience has taught us all our talent, if not genius, for messing
life up. Only the knowledge that God is at the helm, using a
vast rudder that keeps us on course even when we are diligently applying our efforts in an oblique direction, keeps us
at the oars—however "faint, yet pursuing."

11 Evil

An irreversible turning point in the spiritual life occurs when we first see clearly the extent, the power, the depth, the subtlety, and the horror of evil in the world. From that time on, continuing religious growth brings constantly deepening awareness of the subject. Paradoxical as this seems, it is no accidental or unfortunate by-product of the spiritual life that it leads to this result. On the contrary, the deliberate purpose of religion is to bring us to this awareness of the world's corruption and to consequent involvement in it. It is pitiful that the general laity, if we may judge from its chronic anxiety to protect the clergy from knowledge of the world's nastiness, has this matter exactly backwards.

It must be added at once that the more mature a person is —that is to say, the more he has entered into the knowledge of the essential nature of reality—the more he knows the extent, the power, the depth, the subtlety, and the great wonder of *good* in the world. The human race, while unquestionably fallen from grace, is not totally depraved. It is around this point that many pessimists—for example, Nietzsche—make their ultimate blunder. To consider this matter ascetically for a moment, Nietzsche stared so straight and hard into the human situation that the sight drove him mad. God knows there is enough in the spectacle of the human scene to drive anyone crazy, and that if one stares at it all day long it will do exactly that. The necessary corrective is precisely what Nietzsche could not do—he could not raise his eyes from the cesspool now and then to look at God too. However, God is a fact, Nietzsche to the contrary notwithstanding, and looking at him will—among other things—keep us from becoming raving lunatics.

The lunacy that is really becoming to human beings is a divine, rather than a diabolical, kind of madness that St Francis of Assisi always illustrates supremely well. Among the legions of tales about St Francis is the one about the time he was walking along a country road with a companion on a cold and snowy winter evening. The two wayfarers were clad in flimsy garments, they had had nothing to eat since a dry crust of bread early that morning, and there was a castle over there on the hill, with its lights glowing warmly out of whatever passed for windows in those days.

Understandably, the conversation turned to the subject of happiness. Equally understandably St Francis' companion stated his opinion that it would be great joy if they were to be taken into that warm castle, fed royally, treated like long-lost brothers, and put snugly to bed for the night after a pleasant evening's entertainment.

St Francis had different opinions. It was his contention that it would be great joy if they should go up and knock on the castle door, asking for a little food and shelter in the name of Christ, only to have the door slammed shut in their faces.

He thought it would be further joy if, emboldened by cold and hunger, they should knock again and repeat their request, only to be cursed roundly and shoved away, with the great door banged firmly against them.

He further thought it would be the greatest joy if, urged by their sufferings and their need, they made a third plea only to be set upon by the servants, beaten, thrown out into the snow, and had the dogs set on them to run them off for good.

St Francis has a deserved reputation as a mature human being. If his value judgments are different from ours, the very contrast serves as a good pinnacle from which to view the usual maturing process from its beginning.

Most of us came starry-eyed into this world, dragging clouds of glory into a glorious environment that was full of kindness, love, and wonder. The times were almost never out of joint, except for that rainy Fourth of July or that malicious winter when we were given a new sled for Christmas and the snow held off until February.

With these exceptions, childhood was fun. Home existed, offering a splendid place to change clothes, sleep, and climb roofs. It was surrounded by clipped grass made to roll in and trees designed for the building of huts. Food appeared on the table three times each day, and was available in the icebox always. The garden produced only succulent items like tomatoes, corn, peas, string beans. Wild strawberries grew farther on, down by the stream where the fish were always avid for the hook. Utter calamity occurred only when a broken arm forced its owner out of circulation for two weeks.

However, the philosophy of youth which grew naturally out of those golden years unfortunately did not prove to be the best training for young manhood. There were rude shocks when we began to run into a different set of facts, starting that freshman year in college when we revolted against the necessity of going back after Christmas vacation to an uncaring world full of gambling, drinking, and whoring.

After college we did a stint in a glorious war, seeing some things that we wish would not recur in dreams.

The shocks continued when we found we could not freely

choose our peacetime associates either, but had them thrust upon us by economic necessity. Too universally they were petty people, who often proved to be perverse folk anxious to stick out their feet just to trip us up. We were also sadly discovering that people whom we knew, liked, and trusted could often let us down, or even knife our backs. We began to go about the world a little warily.

This was especially true because the same years brought home the sobering truth that it was a hard struggle to provide house, roof, grass, and trees, to put three meals on the table daily and to keep the refrigerator full in between. Even the garden joined the growing conspiracy, running to weeds rather than to vegetables. The distinction between a weed and a flower was soon learned—the classic distinction that if you cut it down and it grew again spontaneously it was a weed.

More to the point was the increasing knowledge of the sorrows of the world, up and down the familiar streets in all those hearts and houses—those same hearts and houses that memory said were full of ease and joy.

In struggle and puzzlement at this whole new climate we began to talk with people older than ourselves, to ask them what in the world had happened to the world. Had there been neurotics and psychotics in the old days; drug addicts, alcoholics, and sadistic personalities twenty years ago; maniacs even then who killed people for no reason? Had there always been sex fiends, poverty, exploitation, disaster? Was all the sorrow, unrest, grimness, depravity, and inhumanity a new thing under the sun perhaps compounded of automobiles, television, too much prosperity, and other items which had brought on social upheaval, or had the world been as evil and lost in the days gone by while we had been too young and sheltered to realize it?

Of course we learned from those older people that yes,

things had always really been just about the same. In their
opinion, based on long experience, one of the outstanding
aptitudes of human beings was a talent for crucifixion, perfected by daily practice.

It was then that we began to study anew the writings of
the ancient sages, and began really to see that indeed the
story of mankind is the story of wreckage and viciousness
everywhere. Perhaps in this study of old books we read the
Sermon on the Mount again, hoping for some relief, only to
have our new eyes see it as for the first time. We saw that the
Sermon on the Mount is predicated on the fact that this is
a world in which murder is to be expected, together with
the causes of murder like hostility and anger. It is a world of
personal animosities even among the elect, who may remember at the very altar that their brother has something against
them. According to the Sermon on the Mount this is a world
where adultery is common; a world of lust to the extent that
we are advised about plucking out our eyes as a disciplinary
measure. Perjury is common in the world, as is blasphemy,
smiting on the cheek, and lawsuits in which the very clothes
are torn from one's back. It is quite a world that is predicated
in the Sermon on the Mount, which does not waste its time
on sweetness and light. The Sermon describes a world so
hostile to virtue that, if necessary to gain its ends, it will not
hesitate to "deliver you up and scourge you and send you to
prison." It is the kind of world that calls forth from God incarnate the scorching words "O generation of vipers; O evil
and adulterous generation; O faithless and perverse generation" (e.g. Matt. 12:34,39; 17:17).

In some such way we came, at long reluctant last, to awareness of the facts of life and the tragedy of man. We came to
have a working knowledge of that cosmic crash which the
theologians call the Fall of Man. At last we knew why God
himself had to come into the world to set things right. He

came because things were so wrong. We realized, too, why it cost his life to begin setting things right—he came to a world far beyond redemption by means of exhortation. The knowledge radically altered the Christian year for us. Christmas became the way things ought to be, while Good Friday underlined the way things actually were.

Faced with the undeniable facts, we reluctantly put away childish things because we knew the open secret of the world. We knew it was full of the grim pervasiveness of evil, pressing hard upon us, sapping us, seeking to destroy us. We knew, indeed, that involvement in it would ultimately kill us, and that the main point was to make reasonably sure we were being killed in the right cause.

However one puts it, those are the eternal facts. It might be nice to live in a world unspoiled, a world fresh from the hands of God, but the truth is that the normal atmosphere of this fallen world is one of fury, bitterness, suspicion, hatred, malice, smallness, and great jangling. So the pragmatic question becomes "What do we do about it?"

Certainly not, as much as lies in us, what the majority does —including most of the secular leaders of this world who attempt to battle evil with evil weapons. (In our justly maligned rash of TV westerns, "right" always wins, it is true, but always with the weapons of power and of evil. If the "good guy" overcomes evil by dying in its cause he is obviously a minor character who has to be eliminated in order to tidy up the plot. This may not be the best teaching in the world to instill into our juveniles, of whatever chronological age.)

There are others, of course, who will have no part of adding to the evil in the world. Their solution of the problem is that retreat from life of which religion is often accused. In their sickness at the whole thing they withdraw from the world in various ways, content in the companionship of like-

minded folk to live as peacefully as they can. They do not
add to the evil in the world. Often they perform kindnesses.
Their failure to add to the world's evil doesn't accomplish
any good, however. The plague rages around them still, so
that socially considered they might as well not have been
born.

The really significant story of our world centers around
the too few lonely souls who, feeling a compelling vocation
to change the facts both within themselves and around themselves, respond to that vocation. They may not like the calling. They may well cry out "Let this cup pass from me"
(Matt. 26:39). Yet they perform their vocation by interpos-
ing themselves personally against the evil in themselves and
around themselves.

History knows the names of many of these saviors, for after
men murder them, later men build monuments so that others
may make pilgrimage there. Recorded history does not know
the names of all these heroes, however, by any means. It cannot possibly keep up with them, for religion produces in
every new generation people who will sincerely say "for their
sakes I sanctify myself" (John 17:19). This has often been
called, by folk who stand self-convicted of a little mind, "the
height of egotism." There is a sense, however, in which it is
indeed egotism. It is the fulfillment of the ego, the real blos-
soming of the self, the love of self for God. Religion has been
endeavoring to produce it all along.

There are dozens of ways to deal with evil and several ways
to conquer it. All of them are facets of the truth that the
only ultimate way to conquer evil is to let it be smothered
within a willing, living, human being. When it is absorbed
there like blood in a sponge or a spear into one's heart, it loses
its power and goes no further.

These are some of the things, perhaps, that St Francis
was thinking about on that cold night. Certainly he, like

his Lord whose stigmata he ultimately shared, counted it all joy to be permitted to be a personal target for evil. It meant that he was real, that he counted. It meant that his was that supreme privilege to share in the sufferings of Christ for the redemption of the world.

12 Offering

A well-known member of an American religious order, telling how she had founded a famous girls' school ("it would have been best to have had both a lot of money and a lot of faith, but as between these two it was much more important to have a lot of faith") and how she ran it day by day, ultimately came to the subject of methods used in dealing with the daily impossibilities involving two hundred youngsters. She discussed some details. Then she said, "My most important rule, however, is to go into the chapel at the end of every day. I have to put the whole thing into God's hands. It's too big for me."

The principle she was expressing is the whole integrating motive of an individual human life and of civilization itself. Life and work are offered to God, whereupon cohesive sense, constructive purpose, and eternal significance are bestowed upon otherwise pointless trivia.

Since this huge organizing principle can only be learned and expressed in the passing moments, it is best illustrated by referring to some of life's little punctuation marks. Such everyday examples also serve to show that the attitude, which in its high development can only be a fruit of deep religion, is at the same time essentially a perfectly natural, non-esoteric one. We see it in operation wherever we turn. A six-year-old boy expresses it when he gives an older friend his complicated, multibladed pocket knife, saying in the words of the headmistress, "Here—you take this and use it. It's too big for me." On a high level of illustration the blood donor gladly offers part of his whole vitality. Lower down the line, the successful deer hunter immediately calls in a group of his friends to share his feast.

On any level this spontaneous reaction foreshadows its complete flowering in a total life of offering—the offering to God of every detail of every day and the offering of the brimming chalice of all one's days. The martyr does the latter when in faith and hope he acts out the saying, "Greater love hath no man than this—." The little child is learning the former when he comes in with his tangled mess, saying, "Daddy, fix this." The average churchman is somewhere in between when he makes a thank offering to his parish on the anniversary of his marriage.

Offering thanksgiving is the most natural part of this whole matter and hence, being easy, is a good way for anyone to begin a systematic practice. However, nothing in life lies outside the possibility of such use, for nothing in life can rightly be termed "mere." Raw material which seems completely pointless has a way of lending itself supremely to purposeful use. For example, just before the guests begin arriving for his perfect party the host, in taking out the last of the garbage, spills it on his shiny shoes. All the energy which will be released in this situation can be used constructively through "offering it up"; indeed, it is difficult to see how it could be put to any other purpose. The host surely knows a person who is sick, worried, disappointed. Each retrieved apple core and each vicious lick of the shoe brush can be offered in his behalf. So can the disgust, as can all emotional reactions. One

OFFERING 113

of the healthiest ways to use emotions is to offer them to God as energy to be used for spiritual purposes.

The same principle applies to our difficulties, especially those frustrating items which are left over when the rest of the puzzle is solved. To offer these matters to God is not laziness or refusal to face the problem. Offering a problem godward is one more, not one less, thing we can do with it. As a matter of fact, offering is an especially important climax to the whole preliminary procedure. God then has an opportunity to overrule our own "solution," if this needs doing.

A person who has learned, through this beginning schooling, how to "gather up the fragments that remain" is well on his way to one of the most important spiritual works that life affords—the willing offering of physical, mental, and spiritual pain for redemptive use. In this connection there is the familiar story of the dying nun who was heard to be murmuring through her torments, "For his priests." She was offering her pain and her death as an intercession and reparation. She was giving these things, which are far too big for us, over to somebody who would be able to use them well. Her own concerns suggested a particular area where the costly offering could well be applied.

The twisted world we glanced at in the preceding chapter brings everybody his crushing load of griefs, sorrows, tragedies, desolations. It is terribly easy to get so lost in these trackless wastelands that nobody can ever find us again. The habit of taking lesser things straight to God goes a long way toward keeping us on the path even when we can see no landmarks. Leaving self aside, this is the most constructive use to which we can possibly put the sufferings and evils that come to us in the fallen world.

It bears repeating that these things are going to come, whether we want them or not and whether or not we know what to do with them. The promise is clear, the experience is universal, that storms and rains beat upon the righteous and the unrighteous alike, but especially upon the righteous. To proclaim this is not paranoia, nor evidence of a persecution complex. At the beginning level it merely points out the historically verifiable fact that such is the too frequent reward of virtue in a vicious world. Of course this is so. The more we conform to the standards around us the more comfortably we will get along; the more we cut across the current the stronger the current will appear. All martyrs, each in his own degree, testify to this. Supremely, so does Christ, who was a martyr only in the sense that he was evil's willing victim and hence evil's sacrificial conqueror. He tells us plainly that "men shall revile you and persecute you and say all manner of evil against you falsely for my sake" (Matt. 5:11). They did it to him and they will do it to his followers, if only because "to be great is to be misunderstood." In this world to be misunderstood is to be a prime target.

The supreme reason for the unpopular and unpalatable truth that the righteous are especially prone to suffering lies in the four words omitted from the question above. Our Lord's full statement was "*Blessed are ye when* men shall revile and persecute you." Here again is that strange reward which is given to the spiritually advanced. They are privileged to be thrust into personal engagement with evil, because God knows that through them he will be able to continue his own victorious warfare. Naturally it hurts to be scourged, to have nails driven in, thorns pressed down, but when these things and all they stand for are accepted and offered they constitute the confusion of evil. At its pinnacle this kind of offering constitutes union with Christ on his redeeming Cross, where the victorious battle with evil really goes on. Religion, we have been stressing, is union with Christ in all his ways. Herein is one of the highest forms of that union.

The privilege of being personally involved in rescuing the

world from its essential enemy is its own greatest reward, in
knowledge of which it is even possible to keep on offering
things after one is tired of doing so. One then offers the tired-
ness. In rare and extreme cases, we are told, one offers up
Nothing. To write personally, I first glimpsed this in conversation with a great priest who was telling me that "we
don't know what faith is until we are hanging on to it by our
teeth and toenails." His familiar history made it clear that
he knew from personal experience every overtone of the
meaning of those words. In addition it was evident on his
face that he also knew that even "hanging on to faith" can be
surpassed. Beyond it there is a state in which there is nothing to hang on to, and nothing to hang on with.

Kierkegaard, among many others, has shown us that for
some, though happily not for all, even the highest level of
seared and flaming faith must be transcended because it is
only the beginning of their vocation and hence of their life
story. God does show, to some but not to all, abysses far
deeper and darker than the ones this book has been discuss-
ing. These are depths that are a world removed from mere
disappointment, discouragement, failure, despair. They are
in the realm of utter meaninglessness; the deprivation of all
concreteness; the dropping out the bottom, not merely of
one's world, but of oneself. Here, apparently, is the real night
and the nothing. This is the lying in the grave and the de-
scent into Hell. A few there be that find it.

This sort of thing is, obviously, on the other side of the
looking glass from the divine-human encounter of which we
have been treating. In this Night one encounters Nothing.
To keep on letting the net down into this utter blackness is,
on the face of it, to have made an act of absolute trust. For
here there is no faith, no net, no sea, no fish. There is only
Nothing.

Each of us has to come toward this, according to his own

measure, for each of us has some glimmering of the meaning behind the rather meaningless words that have just been used. Yet what "this" is cannot really be described further. Indeed, it cannot really be described at all, even by those who have experienced it, because there is no way in words to describe Nothing. "The highest cannot be stated; the highest must always be acted." Christ crucified was enacting this horror when from the depths of the "darkness over all the land," he cried out, "My God, my God, why hast thou forsaken me?" We can look at him to see something of it.

The God who rises after this grave—he does, they say—is close to God-as-he-really-is. Even if there is more beyond, which a yet more purified receiving apparatus will sometime comprehend, this God will suffice. In union with him the human heart can no longer be restless. If a man has offered Nothing, has he not offered All?

Two brief observations compel themselves here. The first is that the real trouble with agnosticism is that it is too simple and childish to be proper to a man. Agnosticism admits that it will not keep on walking through blackness in search of what lies beyond. It finds that Nothing is strong, and it recoils from that strength.

The second consists in calling attention to that tremendous verse in the Old Testament: "And the people stood afar off, and Moses drew near unto *the thick darkness where God was.*" It is amazing that the truth expressed in the italicized words was known in the days of the Old Testament, before the experience of Good Friday and Holy Saturday when God died and lay in the dark tomb.

We return to the more normal experience by saying that the practice of "offering it up" is not entirely a matter of painful darkness, with faith in the reversals that will be apparent on the last great day. Considerable substance of the things hoped for is evident here and now. Spiritual power is the most tremendous power there is, as we are constantly relearning to our astonishment. Each of us has a small store of "miraculous" tales to tell in proof of this point; we have seen strange things happen when spiritual power has been turned loose in the world.

In addition to these outward miracles that sometimes result from the practice, the habit of offering our daily life godward inevitably leads that life to take on a higher inner quality. This is so, first of all, because we find we cannot offer God our slipshod service. Since we are ashamed to say, "Take this unworthy offering," we are moved to correct the ignoble elements that stand revealed. We will not, as it were, give God a broken and rusted penknife—or one that, with a little more effort, we ourselves could effectively use in his service.

Then there comes the day when we see that everything is going up before God whether we want it to or not. Our bitterness, envy, hatred, are ascending as surely as the incense of deliberate offering. While this can be discouraging, on the other hand it can as readily be purifying. We try to cut down on the stench that rises up before him.

A further pragmatic gain is that the God who is talked to moment by moment cannot remain a vague gray blur. He tends to become as real as the wife or the business partner with whom one discusses the events of each day. As real as God was to St Teresa who, when she was pitched into the mud by her mule and assured by God that he "chastens those whom he loves," retorted that this was one reason he had so few friends. The point here is that he was in St Teresa's present moment, which was therefore bathed in a far more glorious covering than mud. Moments that are merely ours are essentially of no moment, being as trivial as the owner. When they are shared with God they move over into eternity and eternity over into them. The present moment is supernaturalized. Hence we are, often quite consciously, in eternal life now.

It is important to press this point that we are indeed in eternal life right now, whether we happen to realize it or not. Eternal life does not wait to begin at some future moment after our death. We will not then be born for the first time and begin to live for the first time; obviously we are living now. Eternal life is, indeed, not a matter of duration but of quality. It is a kind of living which, to be sure, can only be fully savored under conditions different from those of space and time and becoming. Yet the "eternal now" always surrounds the present moment, every so often breaking through to transfigure it. Certainly the present is the only possible time for living. Life that is put off, through refusal to extract the juice of daily events, is so drearily routine that it isn't really life at all. When today is squeezed and savored, above all when it is referred to its proper end, we are living three dimensionally. Time has entered eternity, hence eternity enters time.

Realization of a final level of this whole thought is owed, in our day, primarily to Dom Gregory Dix. He it is who has retaught us that in the shape of the Liturgy lies revealed the essential truth about meaningfulness in individual lives and in all history. That sense-making "motive" for our civilization which we so desperately seek is right here, Sunday after Sunday and day after day, under our noses.

The fourfold shape of the Liturgy is "he took, he blessed, he brake, he gave," conforming to the fourfold shape of the Last Supper and to the same fourfold structure of the Feedings of the Multitudes. Beyond that, it is the very shape of life; the underlying structure of reality. When God has something—a few loaves and fish—put willingly into his hands by his free creatures, then his blessing multiplies it so

beyond belief that the prospective lunch of a small boy satis-
fies the hunger of thousands.

In the Liturgy we are all essentially these free offerers; the
point necessarily takes precedence over our being commu-
nicants. The Eucharist cannot proceed at all, lacking at least
a sleepy priest and a yawning altar boy who are offering
something in the way of time and obedience. Without a con-
gregation to put some offering into God's hands, the Eucharist stops. The priest has to go back home; there is no
sacramental Presence in his village that morning. Similarly
the whole world lives without glory if nothing is put into
God's hands. This kind of nothing he cannot transfigure.

The multiplying miracles begin when bits of life, here and
there, are turned over to God for his use. When a whole
human life is placed in his hands the consequences are in-
credible. If an entire nation should ever come to the point
when—but the mind cannot grasp a thought of this stature.
The essential human tragedy, as Dr. Nes points out, is man's
"denial of his creaturehood, his idolatry of what he makes
and of himself, and his murderous inhumanity." So accus-
tomed are we to this state of affairs that we cannot visualize
a correctly oriented society. Each individual can, however,
make a beginning. In his own time and manner God will
bring about the ending.

13 Death

Our affluent society is crowded with charming, civilized, and "successful" people who quite freely tell us that their entire lives have been motivated by the desires for security, comfort, and peace. They will even admit, in this open confession, that they are constitutional cowards who are deliciously titillated by adventure stories, but who prefer reading them in a lounge chair to living them out personally.

If we take their protestations at face value, these lovely folk furnish additional commentary on the statement "how hardly does a rich man enter the kingdom of heaven" (Matt. 19:23). They also induce a suspicion that our generation is heading for trouble, a better word for which is "blessing," for we have come to great faith in the ability of life's slow-turning millstones to grind out abundant, raw, even abrasive, material for real living. God the Holy Spirit does not easily give up on us, we are sure. "With God all things are possible" (Matt. 19:26). If necessary to save a soul, the whole world could be allowed to blow up. This, the revealed value judgment on the subject, is not too remote a possibility any more. Already the "superstitious" are noting with unease the population explosion that is going on around them. They have the feeling that nature has an uncanny way of knowing beforehand when a decimation is approaching, and takes steps in advance to prevent its being total.

In any case, the conviction behind this book is that every truly human—as distinguished from merely civilized—being must come to himself and to living faith in God, usually through some series of desolations. All of the world's highly developed religions concur. As the center of the practice lie those elements which stimulate and enable the person-to-person encounter with God—prayer, meditation, worship; discipline, obedience, detachment; altars, sacraments, stations of the Cross. The mystical element in religion is always the heart of the matter, and those who have traveled that way assure us that mysticism knows more darkness than light.

This universal testimony, which persuades us that we are not merely involved in the vast egocentricity of deducing grand generalizations from personal experience, is immensely fortified by the ultimate fact of death. Our thesis has assumed the Christian conviction that death is an integral and inseparable part of life; that death is the most welcome friend life has; that death provides the key to the meaning of life; that death is the beginning of life.

While any discussion of Christian living is, therefore, inevitably a commentary on the phrase "In deaths oft," the time has come to look death in the face. This is especially true because overwhelming evidence indicates that the typical American deliberately takes as little notice of death as he possibly can. As a cause and as a consequence of this avoidance, the notion prevails in our country that death is not part of life; that death is an intruding enemy of life; that death is the negation of life; that death is the end of life—the exact opposite of Christian teaching on every point.

So all-encompassing is the American philosophy of opposition to any form of dying that it seems unnecessary to document it here to any great extent. Hints tending to expose it have appeared frequently in these pages—the opening paragraph of this chapter is one such. On other occasions it has been pointed out how our whole climate of opinion is opposed on principle to the various "deaths" herein discussed. Furthermore, the reader knows this situation well from having spent his life in the climate.

He knows, for example, our all but universal desire that death take us suddenly and by surprise. "How nice for him," we say, when we learn how he dropped dead at the breakfast table while reaching for a cigarette after a pleasant meal.

He also knows how we see to it, if that breakfast-table blessing is denied by providence, that death's victim "passes away" (semantics joins the conspiracy) after some weeks of drug-induced unconsciousness and without having been informed at any time that his writing is on the wall. This gross form of theft, which steals a person's most intimate and private property—the knowledge that he is about to die—is not, in America, a crime punishable at law.

He knows to what degree our barbaric funeral customs are part of the plot, as are—since age foreshadows death—our cults of youth and beauty which conspire that no shadow be cast. All in all there is no need to itemize. The reader looks at the advertisements, reads the magazines, talks with people, and therefore is well acquainted with the all-prevailing convictions that living is good, that dying is bad, and that the one is the opposite of the other.

If there is in all this a latent implication that "dying" hurts, it is a beneficial insight. Actually, of course, physical death does not hurt at all. It is living that hurts, especially if we mean by "living" the process of daily dying that we have been describing. To the extent that our American conspiracy reflects this realization it is a salutary thing, for to this extent it is in touch with reality. On the other hand, if death is avoided because it is unpleasant and painful the situation is most unfortunate.

Death is life's most manifest reality, even in a welfare state. The practice of unreality in any form exacts a tremendous penalty, as we all know, but nowhere more fearfully than in this regard. When death is taken out of life, then all the life is taken out of death. We stand in danger of missing life's entire meaning simply by thinking of ourselves as "living people" when the fact of the matter is that we are "dying people." With dying eyes we look upon a dying world. The baby who was born this morning is dying. Like all the rest of us he has the incurable disease in his blood stream.

Fortunately he will discover this. In spite of every effort to hoodwink him, one day the knowledge will grip his personal vitals. Certain consequences will follow. He will find, as every human did before him, that the poignancy of his life is vastly increased by the certain fact of his death. When he knows, in the midst of all those seemingly unending tomorrows, that some tomorrow will not be, he will find an enchantment bestowed upon the today that is. Any finality has a way of bringing up its corresponding gratitude or its regret —"I'm glad I did that"; "I wish I had done that." Death gives life meaning partly because it leads us to look around and think "This could be my last day with my family—at the office—with these friends." Living is very dear when it is thought of as dying, as any athlete knows when he stands poised for his last chance.

In addition to this poignancy, death gives urgency to life; life's urgency is entirely determined by the fact of death. Naturally there are two forks in the road leading away from the realization that "I, even I, am going to die and am now dying," but it is the fact of death that leads to the choice of either. Although most of us vacillate at the crossroad before pledging ourselves to one or the other of the two great human fraternities—those who believe that life is purposeful and those who do not—ultimately we choose. We do so because death gives the only meaning, or lack of meaning, there is. The end of any process reaches back to put this mark on all that goes before it.

In order to close this discussion on its proper plane, it is essential to note that a human being is not built along the lines of the cold logical thinking machine that in his weaker moments he sometimes wishes he resembled. He cannot make the fateful choice between "as dying, and behold we live" and "as living, and behold we die" through any detached process of observation, analysis, and reason. He can, of course, be persuaded toward a proper decision by reading what the sages say about these alternatives. He can be reassured by noting all the parables—in nature, in human emotions, in business relations, in morals, in love and marriage, in social living, in mankind's universal myths where our deepest insights are expressed—which indicate that this world is built around the pattern of death and resurrection. Yet each hesitant individual can make his final choice only after personally sampling both ways and finding the dying way good.

Fortunately, in response to the love of God and in outreach toward the love of man, even the most determined hedonist occasionally samples the exotic fruit of sacrifice, negation, and death. Mankind's hope is that in the experience he will learn that such occasions were, and led to, his most really satisfying moments. Thus he may decide to make a career of it.

Along this road he will be overtaken by death, of necessity and by choice, many times and under many forms. He will live as if dying, reluctantly at first but more readily as the strange custom becomes ingrained. In this process, long before that final incident which is physical death, he will have learned the truth of Archbishop Temple's observation—which uses an expression employed previously in this chapter, but in a totally different sense—that when one lives this way he hardly notices death at all.

At the end of this path he will at last become a self—the self that God intended, that God foresaw, that God loved, that God produced in great travail (his travail, not ours, it is finally seen). He enters that mysterious realm of freedom, of real being, where he can love himself for God.

The God who meets him there is he of St John's Gospel (John 11:1-45), who came after long deliberate delay to the grave where Lazarus had been lying dead four days, who rolled away the stone, and who said "Loose him, and let him go."